Salt of the Earth

Heather Robertson

Salt of the Earth

James Lorimer & Company, Publishers
Toronto   1974

ISBN 0-88862-075-6

Credits for photographs and textual excerpts are listed on page 224, which should be considered as an extension of the copyright page.

Design/Don Fernley

James Lorimer & Company, Publishers
35 Britain Street
Toronto

Printed and bound in Canada

Contents

I gratefully acknowledge the assistance of the Canada Council
Explorations program.

Preface

Among the more than two million people who came to settle the Canadian west between the building of the CPR across the prairies in 1882 and the outbreak of war in Europe in 1914 were those whose passion and livelihood was to record the construction of a new prairie civilization in the way that painters like Paul Kane had documented the twilight of the old. Their method was as new as the railway technology which had brought them west: the camera was a quick, inexpensive and popular way of providing an instant historical record and of giving uprooted people self-awareness, a firm identity to go with a new life in a new land.

Many of the early frontier photographers were experienced professionals seeking to make their fortunes and reputations in the boom cities—Winnipeg, Moose Jaw, Calgary, Edmonton—where money was plentiful and the need for status, for the reproduction and publication of success, obsessive. Almost every little prairie village had its resident photographer whose studio was a little cubby over the furniture store or meat market and who supplemented his income by running a bake shop or watch repair or oyster bar on the side. Some were homesteaders and businessmen who had failed and bought a camera as a last resort; others were gifted amateurs, schoolteachers, journalists, farmers like John Howard of Whitewood, Saskatchewan who made his own camera, developed his own photographs in a homemade tub and left 150 excellent glass negatives as a record of his neighbourhood.

At the turn of the century photography was still a fad, a rare and practical luxury, a means of at once showing respect, preserving a memory and decorating the house.

> We had two new pictures now, enlarged photographs of father and mother in heavy oak frames with a gilt edge, done by a travelling artist, who drove a team of mules and carried a few lines of tinware. Every family in the neighbourhood had taken advantage of his easy plan to secure a lasting work of art. You paid only for the frame and received the picture entirely free though this offer might be withdrawn any minute for he was doing this merely to get his work known. He said there was no nicer way to give one's parents a pleasant surprise, and the pictures would be delivered in time for Christmas. When they came, we all had a surprise. We had thought the seven dollars and thirty-five cents paid for both frames but we were wrong. Each one cost that amount and even at that the artist was losing money. The pictures were accepted and hung on the log walls, and in the declivities behind them were kept tissue paper patterns, newspaper clippings and other semi-precious documents, thus relieving the congestion in the real archives, lodged in the lower regions of the clock, where notes, grain tickets, tax receipts were kept. [Nellie McClung, *Clearing in the West* (Toronto: Thomas Allen & Son, 1964), p. 167]

Photographs were prized also as documents, records to be sent to relatives back east as proof positive of the family's continued existence and an illustration of its success. Most pioneers preferred to be photographed outdoors, in front of their shops or homes, dressed in their best clothes, surrounded by their children and as many of their prized possessions as could be accommodated in the photograph. Thus even formal prairie photographs tend to have a casual, snapshot quality and come freighted with detail and background information which is missing from conventional studio portraits. Simply the effort to keep up appearances—the formal black taffeta dress and stiff-collared suit worn by a couple sitting on chairs in the dirt in front of their tiny clapboard shanty—speaks more than any words about the culture shock of homesteading.

The settlers had an intuitive historical sense. They knew that they were engaged in an extraordinary human event and that what they were living through would one day be important, perhaps not to their children or grandchildren, but to the later generations whose seed they were planting in the prairie soil. Most of the photographs have an objectivity which goes beyond the family snapshot and which gives them a universal, archetypal significance. Photographers laboured assiduously to record not only individuals but fashions, architecture, occupations, entertainment, work, everything from the humblest of household chores to the most pretentious theatrical celebrations. Everything was important. Frontier society was self-conscious and proud but not vain: the village photographers who captured their communities in hundreds of superb photographs were so modest about their work that most didn't bother to sign their photographs or to leave any records at all.

The photographs in this book were selected on the basis of clarity and quality from thousands preserved in the provincial archives of Manitoba, Saskatchewan and Alberta, the Public Archives of Canada, the Glenbow-Alberta Institute and the Notman Collection at the McCord Museum in Montreal. Some, such as the Ernest Brown and Notman photographs, come from the collections of photographic studios; others have been donated to the archives by private individuals. All of the photographs were taken between 1885 and 1920.

The autobiographical accounts which accompany the photographs are taken from diaries, letters, reminiscences and manuscripts written or recorded by the settlers. Like the photographs they represent only a tiny fragment of the material available in archive collections. A great deal of material in Ukrainian and Icelandic is still untranslated; much more exists in private collections. Rural essay contests have produced a wealth of homesteading accounts but, since these competitions tended to bypass town life, there is a corresponding paucity of manuscripts by shopkeepers, blacksmiths or undertakers.

Both the photographs and the written excerpts reflect the values and attitudes of people wealthy enough to have their pictures taken and culturally sensitive enough to want to record the intimate details of their lives for posterity. The conventions are also those of the time: early photographs of Mennonites are rare since the church frowned on photography; homesteaders write frankly about poverty and death but skirt gingerly around sex and violence and emotion, and people who are opinionated about politics evade comment on personal or social relationships. The prose is dispassionate yet remarkably clear, sensitive and perceptive. Like the photographs it grew out of an intense desire to communicate, to explain to an abandoned or unborn civilization the wonder and horror of daily survival on the prairie and, because of this, it has a concentration, an intensity which conveys as much in what is left unsaid as in what is spoken.

Salt of the Earth is a portrait of the rural settlement of the prairies seen through the eyes of the settlers themselves, the ordinary people who did the work and, almost incidentally, created works of art. It is their book.

1

Introduction

Introduction

Free land—several million square miles of virgin prairie in the Canadian west for anyone who wanted it: it was an irresistable offer which precipitated one of the greatest human migrations in history.

When the North-West Territories was purchased by the Canadian government from the Hudson's Bay Company for 300,000 pounds sterling in 1869, it was a wilderness inhabited by a few thousand nomadic Indians, settlements of Métis buffalo hunters, an agricultural colony at Red River and a handful of fur traders. Canada incorporated it into the nation by building the Canadian Pacific Railway; the railway needed settlers. In 1882, as the tracks were being laid across the prairies, the Homestead Act was passed to encourage the agricultural settlement of the North-West. For a ten dollar fee an adult male could acquire a quarter section—160 acres—of farm land plus, for another ten dollars, an option on an adjoining quarter. He agreed to break the sod, erect a shelter and live on his property for at least six months of the year for a period of three years. Then the land was his.

The offer provoked a land rush and frantic speculation. Because of vast land grants given to the CPR, the Hudson's Bay Company and private colonization syndicates who held the property for speculation, immigration was haphazard and sporadic for ten years following the building of the railway until Laurier's Liberal government, realizing that the economic prosperity of Canada depended on prairie farmers as producers of grain and consumers of manufactured products, initiated a more aggressive policy in 1896. Minister of the Interior Clifford Sifton solicited his new settlers not only from Great Britain and eastern Canada, but also from the peasant and tenant farming populations of eastern Europe, agricultural people he knew would adapt immediately to the hardships of homesteading and who would provide a solid, industrious and domestic base for a new agricultural economy in the West. Sifton papered Europe with posters, pamphlets and advertisements promising free land in the golden west, an enchanted paradise of invigorating climate, bumper crops, booming cities and unlimited wealth. Hired journalists wrote glowing articles in the foreign press, immigration agents spoke in hired halls and distributed literature at country fairs, land seekers' tours were arranged for the influential who received a fee for each new immigrant they delivered from their homeland. Swedes, Germans, Ukrainians, English, Danes, Jews — they all came by the thousands. Discrimination was practised only against the sick, the insane and the Chinese, who could not bring their wives or families and who paid a 500 dollar tax for the privilege of entering Canada.

The people who came were the landless—working people, artisans, failing businessmen, tenant farmers, the seventh sons of country gentlemen without property or occupation, reprobate scions of aristocratic families, preachers, orphans, the unmarried daughters of poor but respectable middle-class families, shepherds, peddlars, schoolmasters; the young seeking adventure, the old trying to find a means of setting their children up in life. Some came with money and possessions—Limoges china and silver tea services, carpets, pianos and canaries in cages—others had only a change of clothes rolled in their bedding, but life on the prairie made the bric-a-brac of old cultures redundant and absurd. The settlers said that a homesteader had to lose everything before he could begin. They built their own sod shantys or log or frame shacks, broke their own sod and raised their own food: a man's success was measured not by his accent or possessions but by his ability to survive.

Many were broken, driven out by drought or bankruptcy or despair; death was swift and capricious. Each homesteader, each family, was alone, miles from the nearest neighbour, a day's journey from town, engaged in a life-and-death struggle, an existential confrontation with the land which gave each day, each hour personal significance. They endured. They lived by their wits, the skill of their hands and the strength of their backs, a Babel of races and cultures gritting their teeth against cold and pestilence and hunger, not ashamed of their soil-stained hands or faded clothes, not too proud to accept help from a stranger, building their schools and churches from scratch, knitting the community together with rituals and celebrations and games, repressing anger and hate, cultivating tolerance and order, maintaining, in spite of the pain and labour and frustration, a fierce personal dignity. They survived by unspoken faith, a conviction that they were creating afresh, laying their hands to the construction of a new society which would give their sacrifice significance, a world which would be free of old sins, in which men could live in freedom and equality, prosperity and peace.

It was, however, instant civilization, the compression of millenia into a single generation, the imposition of a ready-made Victorian industrial culture on a land which had known only the chivalry of Indian warfare. The prairie rang with the sound of hammers as towns sprang up along the railway tracks, tiny commercial fortresses where, through the patterns of trade and business, the structures of the old were rebuilt in the new. The wheat economy changed the homesteader into a grain grower and prairie society became stratified: egalitarian on the bottom, corporate in the middle, colonial on top. Farmers found their vision of prosperity shattered by drought and frost and pestilence, by debt and greed and exploitation; the largest amount of wealth fell into the hands of the men who controlled the means of exchange—the grain merchants, machinery dealers, bankers, storekeepers, real estate salesmen and politicians. The extraordinary creative ferment of prairie settlement was channelled into familiar British moulds; the West became a model of the East, yet one which retained its peculiar tensions and ambiguities, an iconoclastic, democratic frame of mind, a unique personality which is the direct result of the shared experience of the first settlers.

The boom collapsed with the outbreak of war in 1914: the sons of the young men who had come west with so much hope marched back east. A feeling of depression and disillusionment settled over the prairies. Many homesteaders responded to the war not with pride but with cynicism—ancient feuds they had fled had reached out over so many thousands of miles to snatch them back. The work and sacrifice, the lifetimes of personal heroism, had gone for naught. Nothing was changed. The war stopped immigration from Europe and reversed the pattern of migration. The West was no longer young; the dream was over.

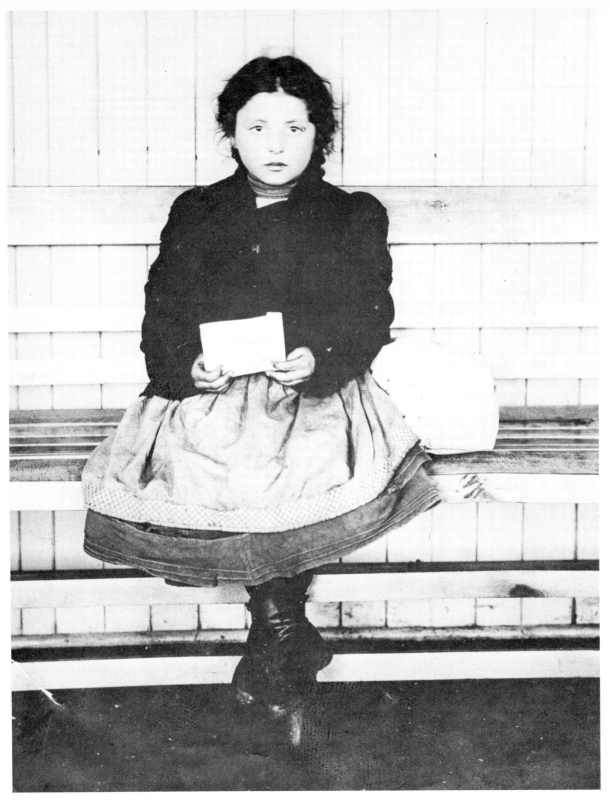

St. John, New Brunswick,
May 1905

2

The Trek West

Ship

The ship was supposed to be a ship that would ordinarily carry 700 passengers and there were over 2,500 of us on board. There were a lot of goods being brought over. Everybody had a lot of things; some even brought their pianos. We were supposed to have a bunk on a certain part of the ship. It was a troop ship that had come back from the South African War. We were in what was called the forward hold. It was below the water line. As we walked down it looked pretty nice, all painted white inside, but when we got closer we saw that it was just whitewash. Later on when we got going the whitewash got knocked off the walls as the waves hit it. The whitewash would fall off in chunks and there was manure under it. It has been used to transport horses.

The holds we were in were two bunks high, sometimes three, all single men. All there was was two-by-fours and boards laid about three feet wide and there was straw in there and a blanket put on the straw and that was your bed. You were supposed to bring your own blankets. There were from 400 to 700 in that hold. It was very crowded. There were all these guys smoking and it would get so foggy you could hardly see the lights so we would have to go up to get some air.

I was pretty lucky. We were supposed to have three meals a day but the first day there were no meals no place. I was just a young kid and I'd run all over the ship and anywhere I'd see a dining room, I'd go in and sit down and I did alright. At the end of the tables they had big tubs of hard boiled eggs—tubs full! I filled my pockets with eggs. And ship's biscuits. With all this I got pretty well filled up. I used to sit up on deck and eat these eggs and throw the shells into the ocean and chew at the biscuits.

The back part of the ship was all holds, and the centre was all married people and they had bunks. They were pretty crowded too. We'd lay on these bunks—the light was above in the middle—and we'd lean on our elbows out of the bunks to read. We got into the habit of hollering 'Duck!' when anyone got sick. The fellow underneath me was sitting reading one day when I got a spell and I leaned out to let go and the fellow across from me just happened to see it and hollered 'Duck!' and the fellow moved just in time. The guy below said, 'Why the devil don't you holler or whistle or something?' I said, 'How can I with my mouth full?' But between the rows of beds they put sawdust, about six inches

of sawdust, and anybody that got sick, that would be just shovelled up. We had quite a time on our deck down there. Every once in a while there'd be a fight and we'd all get around and egg them on. There'd be lots of singing. Some of the fellows played different instruments, fiddle and accordian and all in all we had a pretty nice time.

—P.S. Hordern, 1903, Barr Colony

The Siberia

We stayed in Liverpool two days waiting for the boat. We finally got on a boat that was a cattle boat fixed up with cabins from the stalls. Each cabin held four immigrants—two lower and two upper beds made of plain boards and straw mattresses and straw pillows. The name of this ship was Siberia. An old slow boat, it took us 14 days to cross the Atlantic. On the third day I took sick and was sick for 11 days. My rye bread went mouldy and we had to throw it out. The oranges and lemons did not last long. The brandy held out a little longer. I ate very little and we were fed mostly herring and potatoes and some soup. But the smell of the ship was so bad that I could not stand it. The other passengers were only sick three or four days and then were okay again but I just could not get over the bad smell and kept getting sicker and sicker. On the sixth day I asked to be taken up on deck for fresh air. On the seventh day I thought I would never see land again. One man died on the ship and was buried at sea. On the twelfth night the ship hit something and distress signals were sent out all night by blowing whistles. At midnight we were ordered to put on lifeguard belts. These were cork belts that were supposed to hold a person up in the water until rescued. The people started to panic. I sat up in bed but was not upset. I held my belt in readiness for the final command but the women and children all started to cry. It was a pitiful sight to see and to think that maybe only minutes more and some of us or maybe all of us would be food for the fishes.

—Mayer Hoffer, age 17, 1907

Emigrants for Canada, on board 'Empress of Ireland', c. 1910

Meals

The passengers were billeted in different parts of the ship; first class in the upper cabins, second class next by choice and third, or steerage, the rougher parts. We were in the stern in what had been cattle decks and we were restricted to our own section. The first class could go anywhere in second and third and could look us over. Later we went down into the bottom of the ship and walked its length, meeting some stowaways who had been captured and put to work. One of these told us he had a length of rope and intended to swim ashore at Halifax. Here was depths of adventure we had overlooked. In our quarters, cabins similar to threshing cabooses were built around the sides, quartering about a dozen men each. Each bunk had some rusty looking life preservers and a mattress and a blanket for bedding. Down the centre of the long room was a large table with benches where we had our meals. Our first meal was memorable one of pigs' feet. I have always been partial to jellied pigs' feet, but these appeared hoofs and all, clearly showing their Berkshire ancestry—and salt, ugh!! Soon murmurs of disapproval began to be heard, followed by a swelling chorus of 'We want no trotters.' The steward listened for awhile and evidently deciding we were not chanting grace, removed the pigs' feet and replaced them with bread and marmalade. Steerage meals were apt to be entertaining—on one day ship pie was featured, with which one could carry on quite a game of 'what's this?'. It was evident it was composed of the left-overs from the upper crust's tables, hence one could get a taste of chicken and speculate if another bite was a piece of sausage. On another day a pudding was served—a sort of plum duff swimming in sauce. It was nice and sticky and sweet, but even with my limited knowledge of the culinary art I could scarcely believe a piece of rope was included in the original recipe. The meals were quite generous, tinned meats, jams and marmalade, etc. About 9 p.m. cheese and ship's biscuits were served. These biscuits were about six inches in diameter and one inch thick and hard as cement. We would take these to our bunk and chew away at them at our leisure.

—Ray Coates, Birsay, Saskatchewan

Baggage

We had been nurtured on a diet of Ballantyne's books on the North-West; we read every book on Canada the lending libraries had; we secured emigration literature and pored over it by the hour; lectures and moving pictures on the West we revelled in. Our small savings accounts were examined and checked against the cost of passage and purchase of an outfit. In our innocence we imagined Canadians wore a sort of shooting costume, jodphurs with long riding boots, a belt which carried a holstered revolver and a knife to dress deer (we were rather vague on this process). We compromised on the boots by buying strap leather puttees which we thought rather fetching. We were advised to bring warm clothes along so we discarded collars and got flannel shirts with soft collars (a western touch). We carried a certain amount of excess baggage such as dumbells, physical culture courses, boxing gloves and other treasures which at least made up weight. Packed in a wooden trunk, we wondered how this would be transported when we reached our destination—perhaps we would require pack horses or travois, this we left to the future.

—Ray Coates, 1904

First Class

The first day on board I met two old school friends who were also destined for the 'Promised Land', but being remittance boys travelled Saloon, which we could not afford to do. I would like to say they were the finest young fellows I have ever met, would always share their last dollar with anyone less fortunate than themselves. The five of us chummed together during the voyage and for many years afterwards. The Saloon and Intermediate passengers are allowed to intermix, but Steerage are strictly kept to their own quarters. You soon get acquainted with everyone on board, as there is no formality. Most excellent grub was served and plenty of it. The bar was well patronized, champagne corks popped all day and far into the night, money was freely spent and a general air of festivity pervaded the whole ship.

—Charles Alfred Peyton, age 19, 1882,
S.S. Circassian

Russian or Ukrainian families on board ship, c. 1910

Train Trip

My dear Mother,

After waiting two weeks in Winnipeg and going down to the station every morning to try and get on a train going to Brandon I was rewarded this morning by finding that a train was this time ready to start. I breakfasted at 7:30 a.m. making a very hasty meal as the transfer sleigh came for my baggage just as I was beginning to breakfast so I had to swallow a cup of tea and a piece of toast and hurry off to the station.

I called for Mr. Ramsay on my way down and found much to my annoyance and disgust that he was still in bed and did not intend coming up with me. I cannot help feeling annoyed with him as so far I have had to do everything, not only in Ontario but here, making banking arrangements and everything else and now he lets me start so as to have things a little more comfortable by the time he gets down. This morning the weather was delightful, warm and bright as a May day, not a breath of wind at the station. I found an immense crowd of people. I got some things checked but some of them were put on board as there was not room for one quarter of the baggage. After an hour's delay we at last got off with an immense train just packed with people. Many could not get seats. As I now write I am packed in as tight as I can squeeze.

For three hours we went along very slowly only making about ten miles an hour only having one engine when we ought to have two if not three. About 11:30 a.m. suddenly without any warning a blizzard sprung up and in five minutes it was blowing a gale, in ten minutes a perfect hurricane. You could not see ten yards, the snow flying over the prairie in such clouds. In fifteen minutes or less even the train, which from the time the storm came up went slower and slower, came to a stop and we have not since moved an inch. The passengers turned out with snow shovels but the storm was so fierce they had to come inside again and their work was of no avail as it filled up faster than they could shovel it out. It is now 4 p.m. and the storm is raging with unabated fury. You can't see ten yards. The wind at times is so fierce that the car sways from side to side. To add to our troubles it is getting bitterly cold and the stock of fuel is getting low. We are thirty miles from any village. They say the prospects are even if the storm abates now we cannot get to a village for two days as they will have to dig out the whole line. I was fortunate enough to get one small orange. There is not a thing to eat on the train and it is impossible to get any assistance until they can dig out the road. I have a small flask with a little whiskey which I am sharing with my fellow passengers but it won't last more than a few hours. There are a great many women and children on board and the prospects are there will be terrible suffering from hunger and cold. My enthusiasm for this glorious country is fast dying out and I would give anything for something to eat but there seems no hope of even getting a bite for the next 48 hours. I never before realized what it was to be hungry and Ontario people couldn't realize what a storm on the prairie means. I have over two thousand dollars cash about me and a Texas gentleman is sitting beside me. Altogether the prospects are not what you might call cheerful by any means. Fancy, this is the third of April and there is fully three and a half feet of snow in the prairies. I will continue this later on.

7 p.m. Fire has gone out and the car is bitterly cold, wind still rages.

9 p.m. Prospects still brightening, just got two soda biscuits and the fire has been persuaded to burn a little. Have found a pair of blankets so will make the best of things for the night.

April 4th, 7 a.m. Had a miserable night. Fire went out again, car was awfully cold. The thermometer must register 30 degrees this morning. The steam from the engine freezes as it comes out. Had a biscuit for breakfast, walked about four miles on the prairie and then shovelled snow for about an hour or so.

5th April. A relief train came out to about two miles from here to take off passengers. Walked out to meet it about 12 p.m. last night, found it was not even in sight. Waited half an hour, still no sign. Nearly frozen. Was obliged to return to the train. Passed a miserable night. Fires out. Cold cars in a disgusting state. Smell sickening. This morning is a windy day but very cold. There is still an immense drift about fourteen feet height between us and relief engine. About 150 men are digging but the snow is as hard as a rock and the work goes on slowly. A faint hope only of getting through to-day. One biscuit for breakfast. Feeling very sick and weak to-day. Have a frightful cold. Tavern fare does not agree with me at all. We are not so crowded to-day. About 200 left last night by train. With much love, Believe me

Your afft. Son,
'J.M. Wallis'

Colorado settlers arriving by special train in Bassano, Alberta, March 1914

Winnipeg

The train was full of immigrants like ourselves. Parents with children of all ages, most of them Canadians from the eastern provinces, with a sprinkling of English. As the days wore on children became cranky, babies cried, parents tired. As we neared Winnipeg we ran into a snow storm and the snow became so deep we made but little progress and kept stopping while the track was cleared. We had on six engines, four in front and two behind. When we were still a few miles from Winnipeg the conductor told us we might as well settle ourselves for the night as we could not get through till morning. We had hardly done so when he returned and said we should soon be there, and had better get ready. At 10:30 p.m. the train pulled into the station.

Out we go. Oh! the cold, how it nipped our faces, our ears, our feet. We were glad to shelter ourselves in the waiting room which was full to overflowing. Father, with several other men, went out to see if he could get rooms, but came back in about an hour and said everything was full. The police (they were big men in buffalo coats, fur caps and mitts) told the people they would have to make shift as well as they could in the waiting room for the night.

The next day we stayed for hours in that waiting room while my father hunted the city for accommodation. Late in the afternoon he procured a room in a hotel which wasn't quite finished, but the proprietor let us have it as a favour, as we could get nothing else. We paid five dollars a day for that room and all it had was beds made up on the floor. At first we went down for meals but they were poor and badly cooked. They used to chop slices of meat of a frozen quarter of beef and then fry it to a chip, so we bought provisions and picnicked in our room.

—*Gertrude Winter, 1882*

Colonist car

The railway carriages, or coaches, and the engines or locomotives seemed very different to those in England. The locomotives bigger, with a large headlight, and a big bell that was continously ringing, and a whistle deeper and louder. The coaches have a corridor through them and are divided into sections to contain four passengers each. Above the seats is a tea tray affair, which can be closed up into the roof during the day or used for baggage. At night the baggage is stowed away under the seats that are converted into a bed for two, while the 'tea tray' becomes a bunk into which two travellers can clamber up.

Every car has a stove set up at one end, together with a cistern of water, so that passengers can make tea and cook meals.

Noel Copping, age 20, 1909, Bulyea, Saskatchewan

Front cover of pamphlet prepared by the Manitoba Department of Agriculture and Immigration, c. 1892

Interior of a Colonist car, CPR, c. 1908

Immigration Sheds, Quebec, c. 1911

Land rush

Two applicants for land waited one morning at the door of the Dominion Lands Office in Prince Albert, Saskatchewan. One, the first in line, was a fair-haired, blue-eyed lad of eighteen, the other a man of thirty, coarse, unshaven and very much unwashed.

'You guys got land enough,' growled the latter, menacing. 'D'ye want the whole earth?'

The lad only smiled and turned his face to the door. Two more days of waiting and then the land would be his. He had waited long and patiently. Three years before, he, with his father and two brothers, had settled in the district, his brothers and his father each taking a quarter in the same section. The remaining quarter was good but they lacked the necessary funds to pre-empt and the younger boy was not old enough to file on his own account.

Now, after being filed on, cancelled, and finally neglected by the applicant for cancellation, the land was open to any and all, and our young applicant stood in line, within two days of obtaining his heart's desire.

He remembered seeing the next in line at a neighbouring farm where he had been employed as teamster. Undoubtedly both were after the same quarter. The young lad wondered that the other should remain, seeing that he had no possible chance, but still the elder man waited. He was watching for his opportunity and it wasn't long in coming.

A lady hesitated in front of the building. She asked to be directed on her journey and, in his eagerness to be of assistance, the young man moved a few steps towards her.

When he returned he found that his unsavoury companion had moved up a step. He tried to elbow his way in but met with determined resistance.

'I say!' he cried. 'That's not fair!'

His argument had not the slightest effect; his muscles also proved unavailing. He was finally told by an old wiseacre that he was out of the running and that he had lost his place.

He returned home and, full of indignation, blurted out his story. Father, brothers and neighbours listened in silence. His father spoke first.

'We still have 24 hours,' he said grimly. 'We'll start right away.

If any of you neighbours care to come along, we'll sure appreciate your help.'

They were on the road within an hour—a good half-dozen of them.

The next morning they stood in a little group outside the Land Office. There were now over a dozen applicants waiting admission and, at the door, bleary-eyed and dusty, stood the Cheat. He glared savagely at the newcomers.

The lad's father passed up the line and examined the entrance. The door was solid, in one section only, and opened outward. A transom window, two feet in height, overhung the door. The rest of the group drew near. The father glanced at his perfectly-timed watch. It was one minute to nine.

'Now!' he cried.

Five pairs of strong, brawny arms lifted the lad aloft and held him there, poised in mid-air. Footsteps and the rattling of keys were heard inside the door. The rest of the story is told by the clerk who opened the door.

'It was my duty to unlock the door and admit the applicants, giving numbered tickets to each in turn as they entered. There had often been unruly scenes outside the door and we had become rather accustomed to them, but I was totally unprepared for what happened on this occasion.

'I was about six feet from the door when I heard a crash, and a shower of broken glass fell about my ears. A pair of legs dangled above my head and a young man dropped lightly between me and the door.

'It was nine o'clock. The young man asked me for his ticket. He was the first man inside the building—I gave him his ticket. I then unlocked the door and handed ticket No. 2 to the seediest-looking man that ever entered the office. He went away about fifteen minutes later, the maddest man I ever saw.'

Land rush, c. 1909

3

Homesteading

Homestead

We reached our homestead at last. I'll never forget the desolate feeling that came over me, when, with the contents of the waggon out on the ground, we sat on a box and looked around, not a sign of any other human habitation or a road leading to one to be seen, nothing but bluff and water and grass. Then I realized that we were at the end of our journey, that this was to be our home, that if we wanted a house to cover us, a stable for our horses, a well for drinking water, it would all have to be the work of our own hands.

We pitched our tent and tethered our horses and set up the cookstove out in the open and built a table, and as the days went by a makeshift kind of stable was raised, for we were green, oh! so very green, to the manner of utilizing the logs to make a good building; also to the knowledge of what kind of climate we were up against, for I remember we were so eager for a garden. As soon as a little bit of land was broken we planted peas, beans, radishes, lettuce, etc. They came up and throve splendidly, but one morning about the middle of August we got up to find them laying flat and black. Our first frost had visited us.

A hole was dug by the side of a slough, where the water filtered through more agreeable to the taste.

Then our thoughts turned to the house. A cellar was dug, but we found that the cost of lumber would take all our money. Whatever would happen to us if we had nothing to buy food with in the winter ahead? So we decided to put up anything with four walls and a roof.

I was so tired of living in a bell tent and quite envied the horses their square built stable, poor as it was. While living in the tent we had three days' rain in July, steady downpour.

We managed to stand the cookstove inside the opening of the tent, with the pipe out, but how we lived through those days and kept happy, as I remember being, is a marvel to me now. On one of the days, I baked bread and had just got a tin of hot rolls from the oven, in the afternoon, when we heard somebody outside. It was a man who had seen our tent from a distance, and had come over to see if he could beg or borrow some bread. He was one of three men homesteaders, about a mile away. They had only a sleeping tent and a camp stove, which they could not operate at all in the rain. Being bachelors they prepared one meal at a time, cooking bannock as they wanted it.

We wrapped up the rolls and told him that was all that we had cooked and he started off hoping to quickly get back to the others, that they might all break their fast. In about half an hour he was back again, lost. He had nothing to guide him going back and had gone in a circle, with the greatest surprise finding himself again at our tent. However he made home alright the second time.

We afforded a lumber roof and floor for our house and two windows, but the walls must cost us nothing but labour. By this time there was a neighbour on the same section, who had a team of horses and kindly came to help plow some sod for the walls, for we found that two horses alone could not break the land. The sod was cut and piled up neatly for the walls and we were thankful to move into it and begin to make it as comfortable as possible. We lined the walls inside with match-boarding and built bunks to sleep in and partitioned them off from the general living room. There were months during that winter when the blankets and coverings of our beds were held to the wall, tight with frost. We daren't try to move them for they were too precious to tear. The second winter we bought a small heater and managed fairly well to keep a fire in through the nights.

—1904

First night

We found the S.W. corner of my land on a Sunday afternoon, I don't remember the date but know it was in October. I will never forget the completely lost feeling I had as I stood there alongside all my worldly possessions on the bald-headed prairie and watched that team disappear through the hills. I was twenty years young, a green kid from the East, in the wilds of Saskatchewan and very much alone.

I decided the first thing to do was to get something to eat, then for the first time realized I had no water. I could see the banks of Snake Hole Lake about a mile north. I took a pail and started out. When I reached the lake I found water alright, but it was alkali, not a bit of use. I decided that the water must be coming from some place, so started to cruise around through the hills and coulees, and sure enough I found a spring of real good water. I filled my pail and started for home, which was a pile of lumber, but—where was it? I had wandered through the hills and coulees until I had lost all sense of direction, but luck was with me, I arrived home just as it was getting dark. I cooked some supper, rolled up in my blankets and went to sleep; my first night on the homestead—I figured I had made a good start on my first million.

When I woke the next morning, it was raining and plenty cold. I was quite comfortable under the blankets, but there didn't seem to be much future in that and the idea of getting out wasn't so good. However, I finally decided that I had better get out and get going, I had a home to build and there was no one but myself to do it. What a mess I found, everything soaked and no place to dry anything. I did the only thing I could think of—I started to dig—and by night I had a hole big enough to get all my stuff into. I set up my stove and covered the hole with lumber. There wasn't much room in that hole, but I kept quite comfortable. It had stopped raining and I felt that I had things pretty well under control. The next morning I started to build my home, the hole which I had been living in, I used for a cellar.

I worked at that shack for about two weeks and the only living thing I saw during that time was a gopher, the most appreciated friend I have ever had. He was a cocky little devil and I came to think a lot of him. It is quite likely that in the years ahead, I poisoned and murdered in various ways hundreds of his offspring, but if anyone had tried to harm that gopher at that time, he would have had me to deal with.

—Z.F. Cushing, 1909, Roseray
Saskatchewan

Batching

The weather stayed nice till Christmas that year. I dug lignite coal from an outcrop on the side of a coulee for fuel and plastered my sod house inside and out with clay dug from the well. I put flooring in it and as I had nothing else to do, I scrubbed it every other day and took out my bedding to air every morning. For music I stretched some brass wire on my home made bench and on this rude instrument I played little tunes. I even made verses to a tune I liked, a love song to my absent wife. I had time to read too. My Swedish language paper came in the mail. I had some

'Western Stories', and books that I borrowed from my neighbour. So I passed the time.

My food consisted of white beans I had brought with me, half a pig I had bought and home-made bread. So I had beans and pork for dinner and supper. For breakfast I had toast and oatmeal or perhaps mush, as a kind neighbour kept me supplied with milk. For dessert I cooked dried apples and always there was coffee. I never tired of this somewhat monotonous diet.

Baking did not really come natural to me, but I had watched my wife do it often, so was sure I could learn too. At my first attempt I made the dough in the evening, with the old style Royal Crown Yeast, then put it on top of a cupboard I had made with odds and ends of lumber, where the pan just fitted in under the half-inch board ceiling. In the morning I was surprised to see daylight through a long crack in the eaves, for the dough had risen and lifted up the roof, so I got the pan out of there before it did more damage.

—August Dahlman, 1908, Estevan

Original Roy Benson homestead, Munson area, Alberta, c. 1910

ERNEST BROWN
(PHOTO #161)

A HOMESTEADERS FIRST RESIDENCE

Sod hut

The walls were built like laying bricks. The sods were cut about two feet long, were thirteen inches wide and four inches thick laid with grass side down. We had one rough-made door about six feet high and 2-foot-6-inches wide which was difficult to fit into the sod walls. The roof was lean-to type, there were three windows 2 feet by 2 feet with four lights in each. Being set in two foot wide walls not much light could come in, of course no storm windows. Many cold days in winter an inch or more frost would gather on the inside of the windows.

Inside, it was 12 feet wide and 22 feet long. Ten feet was curtained off for a bedroom, and the other 12 by 12 feet was used as a kitchen and living room. Later a porch was added which came in very handy. Poles with hay and sods on top were used for the roof over the bedroom; we used boards with tar paper on top over the kitchen. The lumber for roof, door and windows cost about 20 dollars. One good fortune by having boards over the living room was the reasonable freedom from insects and dirt falling from the ceiling, but then the board roof had its faults the result of my not fastening it down. The trouble happened when my father and I had gone to the bush 20 miles away for wood. A thunder and wind storm came and the board roof was lifted off and fell into a small garden alongside the house. On our arrival home in the afternoon we found mother unhurt in the kitchen without a roof overhead.

Rough bedsteads were made of poles, the mattress cover being filled with hay, the space under the beds being used for storing some of the boxes that were in the bedroom. My mother, father and two sisters slept in this room. My brother and I had a movable hay-filled mattress cover in the kitchen. To help the sleeping situation out somewhat my elder sister and brother got work away from home for months at a time. The furniture as far as I can remember consisted of a nice mahogany table, two chairs to match along with many boxes which came in handy for cupboards, etc.

Father brought out 22 boxes which contained our small amount of furniture, linens, blankets, dishes, tools, etc. We bought a stove with oven, a sheet metal one which cost 20 dollars new. Of course only wood was burnt then. We had a table lamp and barn lantern, along with candles. The stove was all the heating we had, in the winter. Very many of the days and nights it froze in the house in spite of my getting up and putting wood in the stove many times during the night, the temperature often going to more than fifty below zero. There were no trees to protect us from the wind and snow. Owing to the fact of having nothing for plaster the wind often blew through the cracks of the sod walls. Our wood was kept in a tepee, several loads in each, piled in a manner to prevent the snow from piling over it. It also made shade from the wind when sawing it up with a bucksaw. The prairie fires came often, stopping any trees from growing in our district for over five years after we came to the homestead. Our food for the first summer consisted mostly of wild rabbits (generally some of which were diseased which had to be thrown away—this dulled our taste for rabbit) duck eggs, occasionally ducks and salt pork which we bought in large chunks. We had butter and milk from our cow, and we sold butter to neighbours. I made a dash churn using a four gallon stone crock, and the dash and top out of wood. It answered the purpose for years. Mother had brought a common square scrub board. Of course all wringing was done by hand. We had a flat iron, handle attached, which was heated on the top of the stove. Mother made her own bread.

—*James Rugg, 1905*

COPYRIGHT,
ERNEST BROWN.
SOD HOUSE
(524)   THE BEGINNING OF BETTER THINGS
BUFFALO BONES IN THE FORE GROUND

Jewish Homesteader

At nine o'clock in the evening we arrived in Hirsch. I was never so happy in my life as when I heard the conductor call 'Hirsch'. I had reached the end of my journey and life lay ahead. I was exhausted from the trip and so glad that at last it was all at an end.

Israel and a few of the suntanned boys who knew me from school met me at the station and it was so good to shake hands with everybody. It was dark out on the platform with only a shack for a station. I was taken over to a family by the name of Frost for Passover and I paid them my last five dollars for a week's board and room during Passover. I still had 60 cents left.

After Passover my brother found me a job with a Jewish farmer, a Mr. Waxelman. I worked for this man for 25 dollars a month. In June of 1907 my father and Israel took their belongings—a wagon, a team of horses, a cow and a calf. The team of horses cost 375 dollars and 12 per cent interest on the payments. The cow and calf cost 50 dollars. The wagon was loaded with lumber to be used for building, an old range stove and a bed, a low-rift sulky plow and a few bundles of hay for feed on the way. They also bought a pail, a stoneboat, a pickaxe, some tools, kitchen utensils and groceries. Thus Israel and father went out west. With hope and hardships they started setting up their future home. The first thing to do was to unload the wagon and turn it upside down. That was the first home on the prairies for any homesteader.

The weather was wonderful with bright, sunny, warm, fragrant days to work in and clear, cool nights. The grass was high and the land held a rich promise for the future. People were pouring into the district to start taking possession of the land. Some came with small, young children; some came with quite grown children; some had money, others were poor. All came with a vision of the future before them.

My father, Israel and I each filed for two quarters of land—one homestead each and a pre-emption for ten dollars each. We then had to take possession by living on the land at least six months of the year and setting up a home. Whenever they would get tired and weary of working so hard they would look about them and see land as far as the eye could see and no other people about and remembering the single acre of land they had in the old country it gave them new courage to strive for a greater future.

—Mayer Hoffer, age 17, 1907, Hirsch, Saskatchewan

Homesteader

I was born at Zablatow, Galicia in 1868. I had never lived nor worked on a farm. On leaving school I worked in a factory until I was called to the army where I served three years. I left with the rank of Sergeant, then worked at various jobs in the village and was married soon after leaving the army. I read in the papers about Canada and after talking to others we organized a party of seven families. I had about 500 dollars when I left the old country but had not much left when I got located on my farm. I arrived in Winnipeg, July 25, 1897 and stayed a few days at the immigration hall.

I inquired of Carl Genik about a homestead and he directed me to Pleasant Home.

Leaving wife and child at the hall I went out, selected a homestead and arranged to have the wife and child taken in from Stonewall, then the nearest point on the railway.

We took out bedding, a small stove, pots, pans, dishes, an axe, grub-hoe, sickle and some provisions—flour, macaroni, bacon and tea. George Zeron met us and when we arrived at the farm we had no shelter but a kind of tent made of brush. I had brought cheesecloth and put it around to keep out mosquitoes and flies. We lived in this for a week or two while I built our first log house. I carried the poles, 12 or 14 feet long, from the bush on my shoulder. Walls were built about six or seven feet high, then poles were laid across making ceiling and roof. This was finished by piling well-cured hay on the poles like the top of a haystack. There was no floor. We lived in this house four or five years; we then built a new house 16 x 20 feet. Logs were hewed, corners neatly dovetailed, then walls plastered inside and out. Rafters were straight spruce poles and were covered with boards, then shingled. There was a saw-mill not far away where I could have my own logs cut into lumber. We lived in this house for many years, then built a larger and better one which is still in use.

—Stefan Dragan

Lipton homesteaders

Homesteading

We landed at Halifax and took a colonist train through—one of those where the seats are hard slats but can be pulled out at nights. Dad had no notion of where we were going except to Winnipeg where he hoped to work until he could procure a homestead. However a lady and family in our cabin was going to her husband at Estevan and believed there was still homestead land there, so Dad decided to take us all there.

We finally arrived at the wee station, in the night sometime. As my brother was eight and I was only six it seemed a big adventure to us but I know it was hard for mother. She says her back never recovered from sleeping on the slats, and when I think of the baby who arrived in July, I wonder how she did manage. I remember being bundled off to a bed of blankets made up on the station floor, and there we stayed until morning.

Dad had 500 dollars so he bought a lot for 125 dollars and erected a two-roomed house and lean-to costing 250 dollars and started work digging a well for a neighbour and any job he could get. Most of his work at various jobs brought 15 to 20 cents an hour, without board. Between work he borrowed a bicycle and travelled the prairie. One day in June when Dad returned he looked as if he had been fighting. Blood dripped from his neck and forehead. 'My goodness!' mother exclaimed, 'whatever is the matter?' 'Phew!' came the answer, 'mosquitoes! Millions! Clouds!' But he had located our homestead. Later he went threshing for 50 cents a day which bought lumber for our shack, 14 by 16.

We moved the first week in November. Mother didn't see another woman until the following April. Our room was arranged thus: a bed stood in one corner, another bed (a spring) was fastened by hinges to the wall in another corner. It pushed up in the daytime and a curtain concealed it. A stove at one end, a table in the corner, a cupboard, four chairs and a rocking chair completed all furnishings. Dad used to say, 'Sit in the centre of the room, face the stove and you're in the kitchen, swing around and you're in the dining room, again, and there's the parlour, again—the bedroom, once more, back you are in the kitchen.' However we spent many happy evenings in that room singing hymns and songs together by the firelight to the accompaniment of the coyotes' howling outside in the coulee.

It was really beautiful when we moved out, one of those clear prairie autumn days, mother pushing the baby in the carriage behind a hayrack which contained our few belongings. My brother and I rode and walked alternately. We only had seven miles to go. Dad 'borrowed' the team. We unloaded at the shack and Dad started sodding up the shanty.

Two weeks after we moved out we had our first visit from a Mountie and saw our first prairie fire. The Mountie rode up, a glorious scarlet figure on a fine horse. He asked if we had noticed the smoke. Of course we had. It had been hazy for days, and we knew of fire 50 miles away but didn't think of fearing it. He told Dad to get ready to fight it. After dinner Dad said he would go to the spring and fill the barrels. 'Will you?' cried mother. 'Look!'

We all looked and down the fire swept, a roaring, terrific mass, right past our shack and on. It singed the hair off the horses' legs. Had it not been for the few sods half way up the shack, our little tarpaper mansion would have been swept away. Dad and my brother jumped on the flat wagon and galloped away for water, returning to put out the fire that was burning tarpaper and lumber lying in the yard. The prairie after that fire! Black, desolate, stones dotting it white everywhere. Poor mother. I remember her crying and running around with a wet broom banging out little clumps of burning manure.

Guy McCumsey building home, Munson, Alberta, 1913

Two lady homesteaders, c. 1912

38

Jake Pearson's homestead, Vermilion, June 3, 1909

Breaking

I started out with two very slow bulls and a twelve-inch walking plow. If I could manage to make those bulls travel 12 miles a day, which I generally did, I would have nearly one-and-a-half acres to my credit. I used to plod along behind that plow and look over that 320 acres which I was supposed to own some day if I could stay with it. That was the biggest looking half-section of land I ever saw. I used to wonder if I would ever manage to break it all.

My way of life was very simple. I started off on Sunday by baking a gallon of pork and beans and enough bread to last a week. I would sweep the floor—if it needed it. Company never bothered me because I never had any. Weekdays I was up and had the bulls going by 4 o'clock in the morning, unhooked at nine and had lunch. Every second day I took two plowshares on my back and walked 12 miles to Baskervilles to have them sharpened — back home and had the bulls going at 4 p.m., unhooked at 9 p.m. had supper and went to bed. I did the same thing the next day and the next and the next. That summer in breaking 110 acres I walked some 880 miles.

—Z.F. Cushing

Plow

It looked nice to see his outfit of horses going up and down the field. He had the outfit strung out, the blacks in front and the two grays behind, and they worked well together. The plow was set to follow the horses and not try to run off in some other direction, the coulter set just right. Sometimes Stan would hang the lines on the lever and walk behind the plow, getting a lot of enjoyment watching the moist dark chocolate brown loam soil slide off the mould board and silently roll over upside down, smooth and glossy as an eel, furrow after furrow fourteen inches wide, one half mile long and straight as a string. Lovely.

Plowing

I had a surprise coming to me on arrival at our little knoll. The knoll itself was there, but the thick grass had been cut and the ground was trampled over, lumber lying about, sawdust, tools; pieces of paper and small barrels of nails were scattered around, and over a yawning pit rose the framework of a house. *Our* house, being built according to our own plan! And by my own man. With the help of another, who was busy at the moment hammering on the plates. He looked down at Jack's call, acknowledged the introduction and asked what I could do with a few nails.

'Try me some day and find out,' I replied, 'but just now I've another job on hand.' And I went off to locate a spot for a pigsty. We hadn't a pig just then, but intended to get one, and as Jack said, he'd have to have a home ready for him. I went over to a slough fed by the brook that flowed from the rocks near our knoll where the house was coming to life. And looked around. How could I choose a place for pigpens? Was there anything special to look for? One spot was as good as another to me. After wandering around, I finally chose a piece of ground with a lot of bushes on it. The pigs would kill the bushes—I knew that much—and trample and root the ground up ready for inclusion in a future grain field.

Fred was plowing. I watched him for a few minutes. 'Lines' around his neck, hands on the handles, he guided the plow skilfully. When the share scraped against a stone he eased it. There was a big rock ahead, and I waited to see what Fred would do. When he reached it, he whoa'ed the oxen, lifted the plow out, started the oxen, let them drag the thing around the rock, then started them up again on the other side. A little later they went up a gentle rise and disappeared only to reappear further on. The steady, slow-moving black and white objects, Buck and Bright, widened the strip of chocolate-coloured earth that scarred the broad green land. One furrow at a time. Slow, unfaltering.

—Ellen Lively

41

John and Harry Howard, St. Luke district, near Whitewood, c. 1910

Sod barn

The children and I built our first sod barn. It was only 14 × 14 feet but it was necessary to have a place to put the cow. The job was hard and we did not have hardly anything to work with. We had gotten a fire guard broken and it was from this that we got the necessary sod. The two oldest children carried the sod between them on a board and I did the building. As this was an exceedingly slow way, as the poor children could not carry enough to keep me busy, I made a harness for the cow and made her help us in hauling the sod. This was a little better but as the harness was not very substantial, it was breaking continually and made things very trying. I had a job every evening of either repairing the old harness or making a new one. The utensils I had to make the sod level with consisted of an old butcher knife and the sticks which were lying around. Finally it was completed and a roof was made from poplar poles which we managed to get out of the valley near by.

—Mrs. Ed Watson, Keeler,
Saskatchewan

Women

By now I realize that this is essentially a man's country and that a woman has practically to sink her own identity and take on her husband's interests. For a woman to come out here, and by 'here' I mean isolated spots such as this is, and not like country life would be fatal. There would be simply nothing for her to do. It would be impossible for any woman to fill up her days doing housework, for in ninety-nine per cent of the houses here the necessary work can be done in a few hours daily and in many houses much less than that, so that she would have many hours on her hands that she would find hard to fill. Books and sewing help out but more than that is needed and you can't be out riding and visiting every day so that interest in her husband's pursuits is absolutely necessary. Another thing I have found out is that it is useless grousing over the inevitable. So many unexpected things turn up you might as well meet them with a smile. It makes things so much more pleasant all around. If you treat life as a joke and

not take it too seriously then you'll be happy here. If you don't then Heaven help you, for no one else can!

I think the thing that I found most trying was the unexpected visitor. It nearly always happened on the days that we had got down to the far end of the joint and were making do with odds and ends, and usually when we were finishing the little we had that the dogs would start barking and someone would announce that a rider, or riders, were coming. Billie would go to the door and shout 'Put your horses in the stable and come and have a meal.' I would scuttle around and dig up some sort of a meal and feel fearfully ashamed if I couldn't put up a good meal and the best china and silver, but now I'm quite hardened and just add an extra cup and saucer and plate and let the visitors take 'pot luck' along with us. If there is nothing else they get bread and cheese and the familiar four pound tin of jam put before them.

I entertained a French Count two weeks after I arrived here, and all we had was six eggs, the heel of a loaf of bread and some rock buns. There was nothing else in the house for Joe and Tom had evidently lived a very hand-to-mouth existence and there were no emergency tins of food such as I always keep on hand now. Billie had intended to go to Priddis that afternoon for supplies because we had not been down since our arrival here. When Billie came and told me of our visitor and when I heard whom it was I felt dreadful, however the Count was very charming, he told me 'In France I am a Count, but in Canada I'm no account!' and ate the scrambled eggs and complimented me on my rock buns!

—Monica Hopkins, from Log Cabin and We Two,
Priddis, Alberta

Washing clothes

Our first venture was getting our clothes washed, of which we had collected a goodly store. The boys drew the water from a hole that had been dug by the side of a slough near the house. It was hard but of that we were in blissful ignorance. What a mess we made of the clothes! The flannels were quite spoiled; the soap stuck to them in little hard lumps and they were sticky and horrid and none of the clothes looked clean. How tired and disheartened we were.

—Gertrude Winter

44

*Wyman's farm,
near Bon Accord,
Alberta, c. 1918*

Doukhobors, Grandview, Manitoba, c. 1900

Doukhobor women plowing

'We are now plowing with 24 women to a plow. The women tried the spades digging, but plowing was easier and quicker. They are plowing for the gardens. It is too late to sow grain this year. We have our faith in God. These trials will soon be over. But the worst is, not enough stock. Without animals nothing can be done. We are starting a new village over there. And so we must let those people for the new village have the horses to haul logs to build themselves human and animal shelter before winter comes again. And that means no rest for the animals—poor things. And to give them some rest, we humans hitch ourselves to the plows. All our men are busy; many are away to the towns and cities getting work on railway construction, they to earn money for the community fund.'

Early next morning the women plowed again. A rope runs from the plow and at intervals along are wooden sticks. The women hold the sticks with their hands so as to keep the rope from cutting into their bodies. In front of the human line is a tall, broad shouldered woman of 40, with a stern countenance. Evenly and heavily she strains forward, her eyes on the ground. She knows that such work is necessary because such is life if death from starvation would be averted. So such work is not strange to her. She personifies the philosophy of a Russian folk saying: 'That one who puts his hand to the plow and turns his head back, that man is no plowman.' Therefore, she, without losing faith, is willing to drag this plow along the earth, if she sees such must be done. Alongside of her walks another woman with dull stoicism in her eyes. Closer to the plow pulls a girl with ligaments standing out prominently from her scrawny neck; with wide open eyes, she looks into the blue depths of that cloudless spring sky, as if seeking something there which might compensate for this harsh toil. She cannot understand why things are so, and in her sad eyes is a longing for love and happiness. Pulling on the same doubletree with her, is an elderly woman who at each step throws her whole weight forward; her face wrinkling with the expenditure of energy. Alongside her in the fresh plowing, walk two little girls in their blue dresses. They are like colts walking beside a mare. They pick wild strawberry blossoms and hand them to their mother. Every time the mother looks at them her face lights with gladness as if pleased she is working like a draught mare and not her children. Pair by pair these women pass, as if in a dream. Finally the last pair with apathetic faces of exhaustion—eyes seeing all and nothing. The deep, tearing, muffled grumble of tearing sod, as it is turned over, the crushed tips of green grass and early June flowers peep out from beneath the fresh sod.

They begin to sing. It is not a song. It is weeping; more like a rhythmic moan from the breasts of these women who cry for an unknown justice. And the shining Swan River laughing in the sun, flashes with swiftly flowing ripples.

—J.F.C. Wright

Doukhobors pulling plow near Swan River, Saskatchewan

Doukhobor march

They had refused to make entries for their homesteads. Then came the pilgrimage, an amazing exhibition of fanaticism and guile by the Doukhobors . . . .

Approximately eleven thousand of them, men, women and children, marched into Yorkton 'looking for Jesus'. Travel-stained, weary, exhausted and crazy, they were a haggard-looking lot. Recognizing one of them as he walked barefoot on the snow-clad ground, I enquired, 'Where are your boots, Simeon?'

'Jesus boots,' he said, raising one of his feet from the ground.

The little village of Yorkton was all agog. Outnumbered by uninvited guests, the responsibility for caring for them during their sojourn lay on the immigration officials . . . .

The immigration officials were much worried and much worry weakens one's judgment. A contingent of Mounted Police had arrived to assist them. The pilgrims were determined to go to-wards Winnipeg and the officials were determined to prevent their going. When they reached the intersection of the main road and the main street, police barred their way, turning them on to the main road leading north to their reserves. Perceiving this intention to force them back whence they came, they balked.

I stood on a hayrack watching events with keen interest as I felt sure from what I had read about them that their Russian backs were aching for the knout.

The Mounted Police rode toward them but they opened ranks sufficiently to admit the horsemen, then surrounded them so densely that the horsemen were helpless. They could neither advance nor retire.

Another expedient was tried. A local drayman with a big team and dray was driven up behind them. He stopped for instruc-tions. 'Drive right over them, Jack, if they don't get out of your way,' shouted an immigration agent.

'Don't you do it Jack, or I'll lay a charge against you myself,' I shouted.

'What will we do with them then?' said the immigration offi-cial.

'Let them go. You can't drive them.'

'They'll freeze,' he said.

'They will not. They'll go down the railway toward Winnipeg. Cut off their supplies and they'll drop by the wayside. Follow them with a special train and pick them up. They'll be mighty glad to be picked up and fed long before they get as far as Winnipeg.'

They were allowed to go and were glad to be picked up and brought back to Yorkton. The women and children were shipped to the nearest railway station to their reserves. The men were locked in the cars until morning, when they were once again headed toward their reserve.

—Dr. Patrick, Yorkton

Doukhobor trek on way to Yorkton, October 1902

Love story

A final jolt and a sudden stop. Yes, we were in Hanley. My train companion, Frank Ellis, and myself, Clarence Butterworth, gathered our things together and left the train. It was a passenger coach attached to a freight train. My farm equipment, such as I had, was along with me, as was Frank's horses, machinery, etc. There was no loading platform but with other help we soon had enough ties piled to form a platform.

Walking towards the town's one livery barn we approached a short thick-set man who appeared to have no particular occupation. At first glance one would get the impression that several inches had been amputated from his fat legs, but his face was bright and his 'Howdy-do' was very cordial. He had heard our enquiries so said 'You fellows lookin' fer land?' 'Yes,' said I, 'and would like someone who knows the country to show us about.' 'Well I'm the guy,' said Dad, as we afterwards learned to call him, stuffing his fat fist into a trouser pocket and bringing forth a half-eaten plug of tobacco and helping himself generously.

We started off with a light wagon and team of ponies, a small amount of provisions and drinking water. We drove on and on and were soon past any sign of a shack or habitation. All we saw was the trail ahead, some buffalo paths and occasionally some buffalo bones, all the time Dad entertaining us with his stories between chews or snatches of Clementine.

We were well out on the baldheaded before we decided to make camp for the night. This was near a bunch of small bushes, the first we had seen, and soon we were enjoying slabs of bacon on bread. Next day we passed several homesteaders' shacks; each inhabitant waved a hand to Dad. We met our first rig on the road; the driver stopped to have a chat with Dad and gave us a very hearty welcome when he learned we were expecting to get land very near his own. We soon reached what Dad explained to us was S.E. Sec. 20 and N.E. Sec. 17. 'Here is fine land,boys,' said he. 'Thirty-two miles from Hanley. 'Twill be no time an' they'll be markin' it into lots, then all you'll have to do is count yer money, eh.' We looked around. It was truly called the baldheaded. We could have shot a rabbit a mile away. We filed on these two quarters and tossed a dime to decide which one belonged to Frank and which to me.

When we got back to Hanley I purchased two horses, some feed and enough lumber to build a shack and Frank made a similar purchase, then we started back again on Frank's wagon, this time accompanied by his wife and two small sons. We drove on and on but were truly lost. What we thought was Secs. 20-17 looked like a different country, having been swept by fire. Three miles wide was utterly black. Two antelope played about not heeding us in the least. We felt convinced that we were right and were assured when our former acquaintance Bill drove up to see if we had brought any mail with us. 'It's jolly decent of you,' he said as I handed him his English paper. 'Say, don't you know this is the Sabbath?' he said as he saw us unloading and putting up our tent. True it was, but we had never thought.

Despite the jokes and odd ways of Bill we felt we had a true friend. He told us where to get drinking water, three miles away. There was plenty in the sloughs for the horses as it was only May. This meant too that the grass would grow again that summer and the thick grass outside the fire region provided plenty of hay. There was one mower in the neighbourhood six miles away which belonged to a Russian, who said 'Me no spake much Angleesh' but he lent his mower to everybody. There were already three women in the district and each one in turn came to visit Mrs. Ellis.

The summer wore on. It is remarkable how much sod can be turned in a short time where there is no stone or brush roots to interfere. A garden was soon planted, also a small strip of grain on each farm. The air was full of the sweet smell of poplars, causing a wave of loneliness to sweep over me. Soon I was dreaming, dreaming of days that could never be again, days that I dare not recall.

Late in October the snowflakes fell, first like down plucked from an old goose's breast, then heavier and heavier until the ground was white. Every flake seemed like another flake of desolation. I tried to read the London News that Bill had left but could find no interest in it. With the feeling of one finding himself alone on a desert island I went to bed and fell asleep. When I awoke next morning the grey light of the late morning filtered through the frosted window pane and I realized how like a tomb it was. I thought of the coming months, the round of light chores, supper, and then the long, long evenings, every day the same. Just then Bill's voice broke the stillness calling through the clear air. He had brought his cards for a game of euchre.

The evenings after that were usually spent at one of the different houses at cards or stories or music. Bill had a banjo and Frank a mouth organ. The winter went slowly by and was not so severe as I have learned since a western winter can be. We had several bad storms. One of these found Bill and me sixteen miles away getting wood. We had eaten our dinner of frozen biscuits and frozen tomatoes eaten from the can and had started for home, but in some way lost our track and were obliged to spend the night in a deserted sod shack.

Spring finally came and a new life gripped me. The summer wore on and I had a good crop on my forty acres. The harvest was early so after my grain was stacked I started off with my surviving horse to find threshing in some district near the railroad. I had no trouble getting work for threshing was just starting and soon I found myself in with a lively bunch of men from all parts. The work was heavy but our spare hours were spent in social chatter and listening to our friend Fred play the violin. I had become quite expert on the mouth organ by this time having spent hours practising the previous winter.

The second day was Sunday and while we were killing time, as Fred called it, he told us about a Mrs. Butterworth who lived seven miles farther back. Everyone listened with interest how this young widow had come to take a homestead and suffer the hardships of a pioneer. 'Gee, but she's the bravest woman,' he went on. 'Talk about pluck, and she hasn't been used to it either. She has a certain dignity that doesn't belong to that kind of life but she never seems discouraged. I often go to see if I can lend her a hand but she has a man to help and is quite independent. She has a small boy about six I should say. One day she told me that Raymond, that is what she calls the boy, was all she had, and she determined to give him a chance, and that is why she came, thinking that by the time she had her duties in she could raise the money to educate the boy.'

I was fairly stabbed. Every word shot the knife in deeper. I was cold for my blood had ceased to flow. Finally I gained my balance and I heard my voice say, 'What is she like?' 'She's a wonder,' said Fred. 'Sometimes she seems a little sad, but of course she has lost her husband, just the boy to take up her time.' Conversation drifted to other things but my mind seemed a blank. The following days and nights were miserable ones for me. One night I left the granary where we slept, first pacing the yard in the moonlight, then going to the stable. Was this my Bertha? Was this Raymond my Raymond? No. It could not be for without doubt Bertha was living comfortably and perhaps happily with her father. Yes. It was almost three years since those bitter words had parted us. Raymond would be five now. I had been a brute to Bertha. Poor girl, she was true to her boy—to our boy—was I such a brute that from pure stubbornness I would let her suffer? All these thoughts crossed and recrossed my mind as I paced across that stable floor. Finally I decided I would not let her suffer if I could find her under heaven's sky. I found the granary and crept back to bed beside Fred.

A heavy rain was falling in the morning and threshing would be delayed for several days so I did not need a second invitation when Fred suggested that I drive over to his shack with him. This was just a mile from the widow's and I could pass casually by and perhaps get a glimpse of her.

The following day I started to walk that mile. At first I walked briskly, but with each step my gait became slower until it seemed each foot was weighted with a stone, but all the time I kept my eyes on the tidy shack. While I was still back some distance I could see a small boy and a dog romping on the grass.

The boy was first to see me and came to meet me saying 'Hello. I thought you were Mr. Faulkner coming. What's your name? My mamma's in the house,' all in one breath. It was Bertha who opened the door. She did not seem so very surprised to see me. I supposed she had heard that I was in the neighbourhood. The story I had planned to explain my visit was forgotten, for Bertha, in my arms between sobs, was saying 'Oh Clarence, how did you find me here? I have wanted you so much. At first my pride would not let me go to you as I wanted to, and then I couldn't find you. I heard you were homesteading and that's what made me think to come.'

Soon I had Raymond in my arms. Bertha was clinging to me and I felt a sob on my shoulder, but I assured her that the time for sobs was past.

—Clarence Butterworth, 1904, Hanley, Saskatchewan

George Kimzie's homestead, Crossfield area, 1906

54

Childbirth

Early in the next spring, I was expecting a child. Often I would run and bury myself in the deep prairie grass and weep for my mother. How were babies born, anyway? The present-day girl with her comprehensive knowledge of life was a far cry from my girlhood, where we were literally sheltered from that type of knowledge. Mother sent me two volumes from England, *Advice to a Wife* and *Advice to a Mother* and studying the illustrations I became more terror-stricken but I wouldn't have thought of showing that fact or of discussing it.

The nearest doctor lived at Humboldt, fifty miles away. My husband had notified him that we would need him around a certain date and one of the McCabe boys had promised to take a fast team and sleigh when we would put up a flag as a signal or a lantern at night, and go and get him. But we reckoned without the weather. For three days a wild blizzard raged and we seemed to be cut off in a white world of quietness. It was hardly safe for Duke to find his way the short distance to the stable. The path was entirely obliterated. When the storm first started, he piled hay and blocks of snow for the cattle, to last them for a few days. On the fourth day the sun shone bright and clear. The cattle were let out of the stables and floundered around in the deep snow, their nostrils emitting steam-like breath on the frosty air. I muffled up in a fur coat and was glad to be outside too, and for fun helped Duke pitch hay into the stalls. I felt lighter, happier, as though some awful load were lifted and we were very gay at my laborious efforts. That night I awoke in an agony of pain. Arousing Duke, he lit the lamps and put on a huge tub of water to heat. It was snowing and so no use to put up the lantern. As I was wracked with agony, Duke held my hands and in between the knife-like pains, I would let out peals of laughter in a wild, excited way. Later, I remember Duke, seen through the haze of the lamp light with sleeves rolled up and perspiration rolling down his face, walking between the book *Advice to a Wife* which was propped up on the table as he followed the processes of birth in the book, and actually delivered the child, a perfect boy, who protested lustily at his entrance into the world.

Duke wrapped up the child and layed it beside me. He knelt down beside the bed and put both hands around my face as gently as a woman, saying, 'Christy, I don't have to tell you to be brave, for there is no one like you in the world, but I'll have to leave you to get someone to go for the doctor, for the rest is a doctor's work, though I'll have to take the risk if I can't get him.' He left me, going out into the early dawn on skis. I heard later that when he reached our neighbour's threshold, he fell across in a dead faint. He came back to me and we waited patiently for the doctor, who was also to bring a nurse. As the hours passed Duke came to me and said 'Christy, I'm afraid I'll have to take a chance and remove. . . .' Before he finished speaking we heard the faint tinkle of sleighbells and soon the doctor, nurse and the driver entered. The doctor had to thaw out before he could touch me and when he did it was far worse than the actual birth. Duke showed the strain as he almost sobbed, 'Thank God, Doctor, you arrived in time.' The doctor congratulated Duke on his skill. The memory of that night has never been erased from my mind. I know the meaning of the word 'man'.

—Edith Lazonby

W. I. Wabath home, Crossfield area, 1904

Hired man

July 1st, Dominion Day. I have been with Mr. Hatton for just over a month. There is a Mrs. Hatton, also three small children. The shack is two-roomed and built of wood. There is a large sod stable which has room for eight horses, two cows and calves. The weather has become now very hot and dry, and flies and mosquitoes are a continuous source of annoyance. The latter especially plague me and before the wire netting door was put up I was troubled with them both night and day. At present our daily routine of work is—5 a.m. to 5.30 p.m. Rise, milk cows, feed and clean down horses—Mr. Hatton usually milks while I attend to the horses. About 6 a.m. have a wash and breakfast. After breakfast I saw wood for the kitchen stove and get water from the well while Mr. Hatton harnesses the horses. Then at about 7 a.m. we commence work on the land. This has chiefly consisted of breaking the prairie for sowing with wheat next year, but first, after breaking about eight or nine acres, oats were sown after the soil had been disced and harrowed, while I returned to the trade of my father (he being an artist)—that is, to painting the house. Mr. Hatton disced. Afterwards I did some drag harrowing and later on I disced an extra piece of land on which oats were hand sown, as the drill had been returned. We have four good horses and a sulky plough, a new Deere. Little yellow violets grow among the prairie grass, and in some spots there are minute strawberries sweet to the taste. Behind the plough a pretty blue bird hovers, reaching for insects in the sods turned up by the plough, its note like liquid poured from a bottle. At first Mr. Hatton did all the ploughing while I walked behind and kicked down any sods that had not fallen properly, and eradicated stones with a pick or crowbar, but after a time I did a round or two on the sulky and am gradually becoming more proficient.

This morning I have been ploughing alone while Mr. Hatton went to visit a neighbour. In the afternoon I spent the time cleaning out the well and banking it round. At 12 noon we come in to dinner, first unharnessing the horses and putting them in the pasture. After dinner I clean out the stable then bring up the horses, feed and harness them. Then work goes on again until 6 p.m. At this hour we come in from the fields, unharness the horses and give them oats. Tea is the next item on the programme and afterwards the horses are turned out and the cows brought up to the stable and milked. This I usually do in the evening. Then any odd jobs are done and the day's work is over. I usually end up with a wash and am then ready for bed.

—*Noel Copping*

Greenhorns

We had found that a group of British farmers had visited Canada and had met farmers who wanted to hire young Englishmen. One of these we contacted would provide you with the address of a farmer who offered a job, if you would purchase a steamship and rail ticket through him. This we proceeded to do and were furnished with the address of a man in southern Manitoba (secretly we thought this wouldn't be wild enough) whose letter said, 'Send me a couple of greenhorns by your first contingent'. We were led to believe we would be paid five dollars a month while we learned the art of farming. It all chanced in whose hands one happened to fall—some put in a whole year at this wage. Winters one worked for his board, after harrowing and pitching hay and havesting. Even after taking into account the usual awkwardness, Mr. Farmer didn't lose much.

At last, thousands of miles from our starting point, we reached his home. We were welcomed with a good supper and invited to turn the cream separator when the milk came in. Our work in the west had begun.

On getting up in the morning we found the Canadian boys made short work of dressing. They slid into their pants, looped their arms through their braces, shucked into their boots, and that was that. We had our boots to lace to the top, leggings to put on, a tie to adjust, consequently we were quite a bit behind. Nevertheless, we went down to the barn to watch the early work, after which, another session with the cream separator.

—*Ray Coates*

Bachelors at shack in Blackie area, 1913

(223) A 'CHARACTERISTIC' WESTERN FARM YARD

1890

60

J. A. Spitzmesser homestead, near Airdrie, 1907

Hunting

A large slough that lay about half a mile from the house attracted hundreds of ducks, and it was there that my brother loved to go shooting, taking along an old muzzle-loader that father had brought from the Old Country. He was only a lad at the time, not more than ten or eleven when the family first came to the homestead, and the gun that he carried was as tall as himself. Mother could hear the shots ring out during the afternoon as the hunt went on, and toward supper-time the young hunter would return, weighed down by the birds that hung from the belt at his waist.

Threshing was slow work in those days, as it was done by horsepower and there was only one threshing-machine in the district. While it slowly made the rounds of the settlement, the grain often stood in the stack for weeks, waiting to be threshed. These stacks of wheat and oats made excellent feeding-grounds for the prairie-chickens, and in the early morning hundreds of the birds could be seen congregated about them.

Muzzle-loader in hand, father would sneak quietly up on the busily-feeding marauders and fire quickly into their midst before they could fly away. The excited children watched from the bedroom window, and cheered lustily as he gathered up the dead birds and brought them to the house.

—*Kate Johnson*

Rabbits

The rabbits sat around the haystacks by the dozens. If doors were open they often ran into the house, especially if the dogs chased them. They were so frightened they didn't know where to go. One of our main dishes was rabbits. There was fried rabbit, stewed rabbit, rabbit ground into hamburger, smoked rabbit and rabbit everywhere, winter or summer.

—*Wilhelmina Taphorn*

Coyotes

The snow is very deep now and the sleighing good. Billie and I have been out several times lately. Coming back from Curtis' we ran into a coyote who was skulking along the trail. He was off like a shot, the dogs after him and Billie urging the team along. We simply bounced over everything. The little 'jumper' that we use when we have no load to carry is only six feet long and four feet wide, it simply glides over the snow, no weight at all. With Billie standing up and yelling to the dogs the horses got excited too and simply tore along, no trail of course, just snow and the tops of bushes showing through. We went over everything. I hung on like grim death as we tipped up first to one side and then the other. We could hear a fearful din ahead of us. Baily and Fanny were fighting the coyote and Jock the fox terrier dancing around and barking and getting in nips. Billie threw the lines for me to hold and picked up the branch of a tree that was luckily handy, joined in the fray and gave the poor creature its quietus. I closed my eyes. I hate anything like that but Billie was very pleased, another coyote dead. Of course they are miserable brutes and eat horses or cattle that get down while they are still alive and are bad with poultry and I too should be glad, and I am, still I'm sorry for the wretched animal dying like that.

That is the eighth coyote that has departed this life lately. Billie and Joe have been responsible for the other seven. They have shot them from the house. One of our horses died and they dragged it around with the team to a place opposite one of the kitchen windows about one hundred feet away, then after supper, opened the window from the bottom, just wide enough to allow a rifle to go through. The lights are put out and they retire to the sitting room, creeping out about every hour to see if there is a coyote at the body. It is almost full moon and with the snow on the ground it is quite light and everything shows up clearly. The coyotes must be hungry for they are quite bold for such suspicious animals. One night two were shot. Billie got one during the evening and about three o'clock we heard a report. Billie got up and found that Joe, not being able to sleep, had got up to have a look and there were two coyotes at the carcass. He let fly and got one.

—*Monica Hopkins, from* Log Cabin and We Two,
Priddis, Alberta

62

Tom Bodgley
after hunting trip
west of Airdrie,
1913

Winter

Winter struck suddenly and fiercely. We woke one morning to find the water in the tea kettle frozen on the range, and it was of little consolation to know that boiled water freezes more quickly than does unboiled. Nail heads in the walls were little ice marbles. The walls were of unpapered tongue-and-groove, good and tight-fitting, but not frost-proof. The house had been built with an air-space and tarpaper, but with no insulating material. Consequently the rooms were very cold. Jack built fires in the kitchen and living room and we thawed out in time. Even so we had to saw through frozen bread, shave candle-wax-hard butter, and do without eggs for breakfast, for when we chipped the shells off, glass balls of the whites remained, and would take too long to thaw. I would have put some unshelled into cold water to thaw, but the cold water was solid ice in the pails. The bottoms of the pails bulged and would probably be sprung, and leak, when the water thawed. So we left them frozen—we could chip out pieces of ice.

Thank goodness the water in the well never froze. Even jam and marmalade made things as hard as in their power lay. Potatoes that had ben left in the enclosed porch were like stones and impossible to peel—when cooked they became soggy and sweet-tasting. Onions became glass balls—they too had to be scraped instead of peeled. Jack had bought a half steer from the butcher in Islay and hung it in the porch where it followed the fashion in frosts and had to be chopped and sawed up for use. He swept up the resulting 'sawdust' and fed it to the hens. Milk froze on the sides of the pails on the short distance from the barn to the house, and even in the pre-warmed separator, ice clogged the works. So Jack set it up in the kitchen which made for a traffic jam that had to be endured.

It took hours to organize matters and get dinner by half past one. Nothing in the cellar was frozen. Apples kept perfectly. We figured that the area covered by the house, being so much greater than that of the cellar, together with the depth of the latter maintained a temperature above thirty-two degrees. In our ignorance we thought this was only a 'snap' that would let up in a day or so. It was a cold snap all right, but it lasted until spring came. The animals' quarters were warm by morning milking time, warmed by animal bodies and sweet animal breath, but they cooled off during the day when the animals were turned out and the barns cleaned. The end of Biddy's tail was frozen off so she lost her most valuable asset—her flyswatter. Several of the chickens lost a leg by freezing. These unfortunates Jack killed, dressed and froze solid in boxes in a snowbank.

When I made the bed that first day, I left the sheets off and put on extra blankets. And though Jack kept the fires going all night, next morning our breath was rime on the blankets.

—Ellen Lively

Cold

The house was built, and they moved in before winter set in. It was not a very warm house, being quite large, and as the logs were green, they kept shrinking away from the plaster, making many cracks that the cold winds crept through. The roof was made of boards, put on running from pitch to eaves but the lumber was so green that it shrank, till there were wide cracks, and when the girls were in bed, they would count the stars, and have a contest who could count the greatest number.

But it was not always starlight, or moonlight nights. There were times when the wind roared and howled around the house, when a blizzard was raging, and they could feel the icy flakes of snow drifting over the bed. Well was it for them that they had good warm blankets and quilts, as with heads covered up, they could sleep quite comfortable till morning. But it was the getting up to dress, in the awful cold. There was no loitering about after they got out on the floor, nor did they lose any time in getting to the stove. On some of the stormy days, it was quite impossible to do anything away from the stove, and if any water was accidently spilt on the floor, it was immediately frozen. Mrs. Morrison hung quilts around the stove, which formed a little room and even in there one day, as they were eating dinner, the steam of the soup froze on their shoulders and backs.

—Mary Morrison

Cutting ice, White Mud River, 1916

Books

Life was very monotonous in the winter, and very lonely. One year there were seven months that they never saw a woman or girl, outside of their own family circle. At times the loneliness grew almost unbearable to the girls. Every book that was interesting was read over and over again. Then their father's library was hunted through, but the medical works were set aside as too deep, besides their father did not wish them to be touched, but among his books were found Flavius Josepheus and *Fox's Book of Martyrs*, which kept them reading for a long while. A neighbour sent some books over one winter, and among them was called *Charles O'Malley*. The girls enjoyed very much when they read of the Peninsular War which is so graphically described in it, and they asked their mother so many questions, that she told them to hunt it up in the *British History*, which they did and soon were passionately fond of history of all kinds, and eagerly read any book they could get on historical subjects. The same story aroused their curiosity in regard to the location of the different countries, and cities named in it, so a geography was purchased and the places hunted for on the maps, then the descriptions of each read, so that they were receiving an education though they could not go to school.

—*Mary Morrison*

Games and stories

The *Weekly Free Press* arrived on Saturdays and was read from cover to cover by my parents who had learned the English language at school. A Danish paper, called *Den Danske Pioneer* and published in Omaha, Nebraska, kept them in touch with news from the homeland.

Wallpaper was out of the question, so old newspapers were saved and pasted on the walls to cover the cracks and keep out the cold. Pictures, from magazines that had literally been read to pieces, were used too, and my sister tells how as a tiny girl one of these puzzled her. It was a Pears' Soap advertisement and depicted a seedy-looking, unkempt individual seated at a table, a pen in one grimy hand. In front of him lay a sheet of paper on which he had scribbled the following testimonial—'Gentlemen: I used your soap twenty years ago, and have used no other since.'

Chess and checkers had been brought from the Old Country and many a long, winter evening they kept the family occupied; father joining in the games and acting as instructor. On the back of the checker-board, was another game, called fox-and-hounds, in which a red button was relentlessly pursued by three of another colour, usually brown or gray. The object of the chase being of course, to corner the 'fox'.

When these games failed to fascinate, the youngsters turned to playing farmyard and spent the time trading horses, cows and pigs. Shoe-boxes made stables and barns, and around them were grouped pens containing the livestock. The animals in these enclosures were paper cut-outs, sent from Denmark by grandma, and had been patiently pasted on cardboard by mother. Buttons from mother's button-bag served the purpose too, and were sorted according to size and colour, large white ones being used for sheep, while little ones of various colours became calves, colts or poultry.

Often, as the short winter day drew to a close, the family gathered round the fire (for the house was none too warm) and the children would listen intently to father as he told stories of Denmark's heroes, or tales of Vikings bold. These and Norse sagas were repeated again and again, until the childish listeners knew them almost by heart, but oft telling never seemed to rob them of their charm. Frequently, the twilight hour was given over to music, and father, who had a fine voice, sang the hymns and songs that he and mother had learned to love. Often, he would bring out his mouth-organ and play lively, rollicking tunes, keeping time gaily with his foot as he played. The recital over, mother lit the lamp and placed supper on the table.

—*Kate Johnson*

Mr. and Mrs. Les Johnson, Enchant, Alberta, 1909

Blizzard

This is our third winter and it has started in with heavy falls of snow and a great deal of wind. The frost is severe too—right through the winter it continues.

My father and one hired man, a young Englishman, had been hauling wood from the bush six miles away every day that it was fit.

Load upon load they hauled with our oxen, Bob and Bill. Laborious work but necessary. My sister and I did most of the chores to enable them to haul as much wood as possible.

February seemed a trifle milder and one day, a fateful and memorable one, my father and the man started out as usual for the bush.

The morning was still and calm but towards noon the snow began to fall and the wind rose. It gained in power until I'm sure it blew with a velocity of sixty miles per hour, a blizzard the equal of which I have never seen since and hope never to see again.

The day went on—the cattle we wintered outside were in the shelter of the sheds and straw stacks. We had two cows in the stable. They must be fed, watered and milked. We began to be anxious about father and the man.

Towards five o'clock in the afternoon my sister and I lit the lantern and did the milking and fed and watered the cows. We carried the water from the well, struggling against that awful storm. Fortunately the well was not frozen. That done, we took the milk to the house where mother was waiting, hoping that father had not left the bush but was there in its friendly shelter. We carried in wood and water and sat down to wait . . . .

We slept at intervals consumed with anxiety.

The storm raged on—great drifts of snow had accumulated around the barn and out-buildings.

Morning brought no relief. The wind seemed even higher. We did the chores as before excepting that the well had frozen and we had to give the cows snow to lick. The morning of the third day dawned clear and cold but peaceful.

Still no sign of father.

We feared he had started out in the storm and that both he, the man and their load lay somewhere between the bush and our home.

My sister and I went over to our nearest neighbours a mile away and told them we were afraid our father and the man had been lost in the blizzard. They in their turn told the other settlers around. Soon men were out driving along the trail leading to the bush but not a sign of anything was to be seen. Nothing but snow, pitiless and cruel.

We lived through the winter somehow.

Our neighbours were more than kind and we can never forget or repay those dear people for their help and sympathy in those dark days.

Spring came at length. The snow went early that year. The flat prairie was bare by the third week in March, but in the ravines and bluffs it still lingered and in a deep gully two miles from our home they found father, our man, the oxen and the load of wood.

They had got off the road into the ravine and had perished there. The neighbours carried them home reverently and tenderly.

Our missionary came and stayed with us until the day set apart when we should lay them to rest. There were no cemeteries then so we chose a spot high up in a field overlooking our house and the surrounding country . . . .

We stayed on the farm five years after that.

Fire

Sunday, February 29 was a beautiful day. In the afternoon two of our nearest neighbours came to tea and remained the night. The wind rose and Monday morning was cold and rough. We breakfasted about half-past seven and my husband started with the oxen to fetch some hay. I was preparing for washing and as we had to melt snow it was necessary to have a tub filled with water beforehand. This most fortunately was done for before the breakfast table was cleared the little girls, who were upstairs, startled us with a cry that the roof was on fire. I rushed up to see the flames creeping steadily but surely down the rafters. To send the eldest boy after his father was my first action, though I was almost afraid the deep snow would prevent his overtaking him. My sister bringing some water I dashed it over the burning place as well as it could but much of it returned like a shower bath. When the third bucket of water was being brought up the stairs gave way. This was a dreadful catastrophe and seeing that no amount of water inside could stay the flames, and that my husband could not possibly return for nearly an hour, I at once began giving some of the things down to my sister who, with the help of the eldest girl, carried them outside, as well as many of the smaller things downstairs. They worked quickly and well taking out the pictures and many breakable things without accident while I was imprisoned up above where I contrived to get down all the boxes, slipping them down with a cord and throwing down a number of bags of flour. How I moved so many heavy things I can hardly tell for my hands were painfully cold and all my clothes frozen stiff as if starched.

The wind continued to rise and the fire spread with wonderful rapidity. Before my husband's return the roof was falling in so after he had taken down the two remaining boxes which contained some china I valued and a barrel of pork which I could not move alone, I jumped down to see what could be taken out from below. I had taken it so quietly and had been working so systematically that I was horrified a few minutes later to see the burning floor dropping on the things below and so much still to be saved. We dragged out the beds and a few other things but as we were beginning to empty three very large boxes the lower floor was beginning to burn so we were reluctantly obliged to leave them to burn. The dry lumber burned like matches and soon the beams were falling too. The cold was intense and the poor children had been terrified at the flames. They had only their indoor clothes on so we now wrapped the little ones up in some rugs and a buffalo robe putting them in as sheltered a spot as possible. All that was saved was strewn in all directions and the sparks had to be continually stamped out. When we had put all we could in safety I remembered my large tin trunk. Now my husband dragged it out and then with his axe as quickly as possible got out four windows while we could only stand and watch the many things still left inside burning. Oh it was terrible! The heat of the flames was scorching while the wind was so cold that I felt paralyzed as if I could not move another thing, however precious. Just then we noticed my tin trunk smoking, so pulling it away from the rest we opened it and found everything down one side smouldering, which the wind immediately fanned into a flame.

For three hours we stood outside that burning building. Not a drop of water! It seemed to me as if no human beings were left in the world but ourselves. The misery and desolation of those hours is beyond words. Everything saved was scattered by the wind over the snow which the heat of the flames had melted round. The books and many other things saved from the flames were spoiled by the mud. My husband left us to watch the stable while he went for the oxen and sleigh. When he returned we collected all we thought most requisite and as soon as the load was ready we took one more look at the charred remains of our little home and feeling satisfied that there was no more danger of the fire spreading we put the children into the sleigh and wrapped them up for they looked pitifully cold and forlorn. I feel sure no gypsy family ever looked more truly wretched than we did, as with something in each hand we climbed into the wagon box on the sleigh.

Silence

Not another building marred the perfect white of the landscape, for the snow was on the ground and it was possible to see for many miles in every direction. Can you imagine being able to hear silence? I have stood outside, alone, and listened—absolute quiet prevailed. It filled the air. It was, I think, like the Garden of Eden must have been.

Christmas

When the winter arrived with deep snow and cold weather the boys realized we had nothing to celebrate Christmas. We drew lots to see who would drive the oxen and sleigh to Birtle, the nearest place it could be procured, to buy a five-gallon jug (nearly 100 miles round trip). As two plum puddings had arrived from the Old Sod, with some other delicacies, we figured we would be able to commemorate that festive occasion. I never will forget that Christmas night. We invited a young fellow who was located not far away to join our party, but he would drink nothing stronger than water. The boys would not stand for that and held him down on the floor, pried his mouth open with the stove lifter, drenching him with a cup of the fiery liquid. In the morning when I crawled out from under the table, half frozen as the fire had long gone out, I found our guest gone. The shack was in a terrible state, everything turned upside down, with part of the stove broken. However we all agreed that the Christmas celebration had been a great success.

—*Charles Alfred Peyton, 1882,*
Russell, Manitoba

First Christmas

Preparations for the great day started as soon as evenings grew dark and cold early and the little children of the house could be sent to bed in time to give the older members a chance to do sewing without being seen and questioned. Our nearest store was 165 miles away and buying was entirely out of the question. There was no mail service and would be none till spring so if there was to be any toys or games they must be made by hand. With both tools and material being scarce my sister and I resorted to the rag bag, for, as she said 'We just have to have Christmas and the little girls must have dolls without suspecting anything about them. The best of it is the surprise.' Mother gave us leave and we two girls clipped and sewed the pretty pieces from the rag bag till we had fashioned three good dolls, one blue, one red and one red plaid, every whit hand-made out of rags. Even the heads were of white cotton with eyes, nose, mouth, etc. sewed in black cotton thread.

Father and mother planned to surprise us also. I think it could not be easily done when the whole family lives in a 12 by 24 sod shanty with only curtain partitions. Of course we all hung up our stockings on Christmas Eve, just for fun. My elder sister had told me about the dear old myth, as she called it, and that I was old enough to know the truth and we must not be disappointed because we did not get anything. So we all wakened very early in the cold frosty darkness and felt around for our stockings just to pretend, but were surprised to find real surprises. In each of our stockings were a little parcel of real raisins and three cookies. We two oldest girls had very pretty little gold brooches and the three younger ones their dolls. Beautiful? Of course they thought so and mother said they were much better than boughten ones for they would not break.

When we had eaten our cookies and raisins and emphatically decided we were having a very happy Christmas we cuddled down again until our teeth stopped chattering. Then we all got up, lit the fire and got breakfast as a Christmas present to our parents and they very obligingly stayed asleep till we were ready. After breakfast, dishes washed, floor swept and general chores done, the sun came out nice and bright and we went for a sleigh ride with the white oxen, Brisk and Lively, while mother stayed home and prepared dinner. Oh what a dinner! Roasted prairie chicken with dressing and gravy, potatoes mashed with butter in plenty and such a pudding boiled in a cloth, with real raisins and butter instead of suet (suet had been sent for in November but did not arrive until February), dried Saskatoon berries instead of currants and several other substitutes but the pudding was real good. We had a lovely drive and got back as hungry as hunters, so it was all good.

After dinner, the first meal on a real table in the West (father had finished making the table on Christmas day in the forenoon) we washed dishes and cleared up a little and it was evening already. We sat around the blazing wood fire and mother sang to us for some time. Then father told us several stories, or rather one story from several viewpoints. In our minds there is still the firelight picture and the remembrance of the story of the shepherds watching their flocks by night, of the wise men with their gifts so valuable, of the wicked King Herod who was so jealous of his poor kingdom and the dear little Babe in the manger. That first Christmas! Although some may think we were

70

then in a wilderness, and truly it was, but not God forsaken, no we thought it almost Heaven.

Danish Christmas

There would be no concerts or childrens' entertainments of any kind for school closed the end of October, and the only church in the village was the German Lutheran which the children could not attend because of language difficulties. This meant that anything in the nature of Christmas cheer would have to be provided by the home itself.

No fir trees grew in that part of the country so several days before the holiday a poplar was brought in from the prairie and set in the wooden stand that grandpa had made. Next the branches were covered with strips of green paper, and when this had been accomplished, the children were delighted with the result of mother's handiwork.

Bought decorations were out of the question, even if they could be had at the little village store, but mother had saved bits of coloured paper during the summer and fall, and with these she did wonders. Almost-forgotten kingergarten lessons were recalled, and they resulted in dainty paper baskets that served as receptacles for nuts, candy and raisins, as they dangled from the tree. Tiny cornucopias too took shape, and brightened the branches from which they hung. Meanwhile, the older children, armed with scissors and paste, converted coloured pages from old magazines into paper chains that were varied here and there with tinfoil from grandpa's tobacco.

A parcel that arrived a few days before Christmas from one of the mail-order houses contained among other things some coloured candles; but the problem of how to fasten them to the tree had still to be solved, and at this point, grandpa came to the rescue. With an old pair of shears and a piece of shiny, new tin, he produced holders that not only held the candles securely but also fastened them to the tree. And, then, from the same sheet of tin, he cut what to the children seemed the most beautiful thing they had ever seen—a big star. This he fastened to the top of the tree, where it sparkled and shone like the purest silver, reflecting the light of the candles, and brightening the whole room. Christmas cookies with holes in the centre were hung to the branches by bits

William Wigg home, Lewisville, Alberta, c. 1900-1905

71

of string, and added the final touch to the decorations.

Danish children have never heard about Santa Claus, but receive their gifts on Christmas Eve from the 'Jule Nyssa' (the Christmas brownie) who, they are told, decorates the tree and brings the pretty playthings. So, when my brothers and sisters hurried in from the bedroom where they had been impatiently waiting, they were greeted by the sight of the lighted tree, while on the table nearby lay a gift for each, games or toys for the boys, and dolls for the girls. The dolls were accompanied by tiny, wooden cradles made by grandpa, and fitted out with sheets and pillows, the work of mother's hands.

There was some candy and an apple for each too, and these had been kept hidden in the trunk since their arrival from the village. But the apples had announced their presence in the house by filling the room with their aroma, and the children, eagerly awaiting this unusual treat, thought that Christmas Eve would never come.

During the evening, the big book of Bible-stories that had been brought from the Old Country, was taken down from the shelf, and father read aloud the familiar Christmas story, after which, all joined in singing carols and Christmas hymns. 'Stille Nat' ('Silent Night') the favourite of everyone, was sung first. At the conclusion of the song-fest all retired, the children being almost too excited to sleep.

Next day, after having been stuffed with prunes, apples and raisins in true Danish style, the goose was put into the oven, and soon savoury smells filled the house, whetting the appetite. Later, when they gathered round the table, the big, beautifully-browned bird, bursting with stuffing was carried in on a platter and set down, surrounded by bowls of mashed potatoes, gravy and pickled beets. No wonder the children declared they had the best Christmas dinner in the whole land.

Sheets of coloured cut-outs from Denmark kept the children busy the next few days, and mother too came in for her share of the pasting and cutting. After the figures had been mounted on cardboard, the paste was allowed to dry. Then they were neatly cut out, and supplied with props behind to make them stand erect. What a pretty sight they presented, when the work was finished, and groups of dainty dolls stood at one end of the table, while long lines of soldiers, both mounted and on foot, were massed in battle-array at the other.

I must not forget to mention the big jumping-jack that always came with the cut-outs. After being pasted and cut out, he was completed by father, who attatched the arms and legs with string. Even the baby laughed and crowed when the funny-looking fellow jumped up and down, wagging his tongue, whenever the cord was pulled.

Every year, the breast-bone of the goose was dried and carefully scraped until perfectly clean. Then, by means of a piece of string, a small, flat stick of wood, and a bit of softened shoemaker's wax, it became a living thing that leaped wildly about the floor, causing the youngsters to shriek with delight.

—*Kate Johnson*

Christmas dinner

The day before Christmas, one of the Hoosier boys came over and told Stan and me his mother wanted us to come over for Christmas dinner. Though we hadn't expected anything like this, we accepted the invitation thankfully. Stan said, 'This is going to be different than going to another bachelor's shack. We'll have to dress up and watch our manners for a change. Do you suppose we should take her a present?' 'I am not sure,' I said, 'just what is proper, but I don't see what we can do about it. We could dress a couple of cockerels and take them with us. She might like it, and then again she might not. A fellow has to be careful about things like that. She told me some time ago she missed her sweet potatoes she used to have before she came here. That would be something she would be pleased with. But I wouldn't know a sweet potato if I saw one, and that store just starting up is not likely to have any in stock and it is too late in the day to find out.'

Our hostess had eight of us fellows from around the neighbourhood that day for dinner, and along with her own two boys we made quite a gang to feed. She didn't have a lot of the things that generally go with Christmas dinner, but she made up for that in the way she prepared what she did have, for she was an excellent cook.

She had an organ and the younger of her boys was beginning to be interested in a violin. We sang songs and told stories, twisted wrists, Indian wrestled, skinned the cat on the broom handle, and being Christmas time our thoughts went back to memories of home and the funny things that happened in our

72

childhood days. Altogether among ourselves we created quite a good Christmas spirit. Before leaving for home we gathered around in a circle with our hostess in the centre and sang 'She's a Jolly Good Lady', and that pleased her more than any presents we might have brought her.

Outpost of Empire

It was nearly Christmas time; the snow was piled high around the shack and a passageway had to be dug to the door. We were eagerly looking forward to the arrival of the Christmas mail from England . . . . What a sack! Plum puddings, mincemeat in water-proof paper, a Christmas cake covered with marzipan, a white satin dress trimmed with gold braid (where will I wear it, thought I ruefully), hand knitted stockings, the *London Illustrated News*, tea, coffee and Stilton cheese were some of the contents. I danced around in excitement. Then we sat down to dinner. I, resplendent in the satin dress and Duke wearing the sweater which I had tied a satin cummerbund around for sheer nonsense. In spite of our elation, we could not help but feel a little homesick for our own people. We discussed the matter as to how we would spend Christmas Day. I suggested we invite all the boys within a radius of several miles who were 'batching' it for dinner. We planned to go after wild duck and prairie chicken the next day and kill two birds with one stone as it were, by issuing the invitations at the same time.

The next day was spent in preparation. I tied an apron around Duke and put him to work dressing the ducks. I made individual mince pies, polished the silver, pressed the linen and wished fervently for some flowers. An idea struck me. My last summer's hat and wreath of roses on it! Using a single small rose and a leaf, I made eleven boutonnières, to place at each plate.

I awoke Christmas morning with the feeling I was listening to church bells pealing and felt bewildered for a moment when my eye caught sight of a heavy stocking pinned on the heavy brocade curtain at the foot of the bed. Dear, thoughtful Duke! He always understood my childish delight in customs. The stocking was filled with odd little things but down in the toe was a red velvet case which contained a lavallière of turquoise and pearls. It was from Duke's mother and he had hidden it as a surprise.

After breakfast I began my preparations. First the Christmas pudding was put on to steam, then the ducks stuffed and put in the oven to roast and soon the air was redolent with delicious odours. I brought out the linen and silver, spread the fine linen cloth, placed the boutonnière at each plate, donned my prettiest dress of wine-coloured silk and was in a fever of excitement. I thought, crazily perhaps, 'Here in a little outpost of the Empire, we must celebrate befittingly.' Around noon I could see the sleighs coming from different directions and hear the tinkle of sleighbells. The first to arrive were the McCabe boys—all six of them. They were fine upstanding young fellows, wearing sheepskin coats and caps. They seemed shy at first but the ice was soon broken on the arrival of Harry and Jim. Their cheery greeting to 'Dook and Lady' (the name stuck during our stay on the prairie), and the 'Merry Christmas to all' made us feel gay, and with the arrival of Jack Durham, the good cheer was general. Duke and I twinkled at one another realizing that this was our first dinner party and all the guests really strangers to us.

The pièce de résistance was, of course, the Christmas pudding. The brandy was poured over, then lighted in solemn ritual; the men's faces like earnest little boys, with the brave little flower in their buttonholes. Later, when the china was washed by several willing hands, we sat around and told stories.

That first Christmas was a perfect gem in a strange setting—the well appointed table in the little sod house, the men guests all so different in background, the little roses in their buttonholes, the genuine good fellowship and the underlying feeling of all Britishers that 'We're a part of the Empire wherever we are.' We sang carols around the glow of the stove, the room lit with the soft light of a lamp and the harmony of the voices was really beautiful as they sang.

We felt as we raised our glasses to 'Home, God bless them all' that we were indeed blest to have such real people for neighbours in our new life among them.

—*Edith Lazonby*

The St. Johns I: Diary of a homesteader

1902

March 30 Easter Sunday, a beautiful day—goodbyes are said and we set out from the States for our destination in what is to be our land of adoption, Canada.

April 1 It was arranged that I should remain in Omaha until Seward had provided at least some kind of shelter, but after the cars had left, I realized that my place was in Canada and not in Omaha, so unbeknown to Seward, I leave on the 8 p.m. train for Milestone, Canada.

April 3 Arrive at Milestone 4 p.m. Great deal of snow on the ground.

April 6 Our cars arrive at Milestone.

April 9 On orders from the Superintendent at Moose Jaw (Mr. Milestone), our cars were placed on the rear of a freight train and moved 12 miles northwest to our location, marked only by milepost 35. There is no siding, spikes are drawn, the rails in turn are swung to one side, and our cars are pushed out on to the prairie, where they will remain until a siding is built. Thus began the town of Wilcox. And here, near the railway tracks our tent 9 × 12 feet is pitched.

April 12 Seward goes to Regina to buy gasoline so we can use the two-burner stove we brought with us.

April 14 Seward returns 8 p.m. He could find only one gallon of gasoline in Regina and the price was 75 cents. The purchase of which would reduce our cash capital of $2.35 to $1.60, so I will continue to use the community stove in the bachelors' tent until we can get some lumber.

April 16 Warmer—finish unloading car. I churn two lbs. of butter, gather two eggs. While doing my work, a handcar with two men aboard arrived, and seeing our tent, came over. One of them proved to be R. H. Williams of Regina. He enquired what was going on. I told him it was a new colony of homesteaders just arrived to start a new town. When he found I was the only woman in the colony, he insisted I should accompany him to Regina and stay at their home until we had become settled but I refused, feeling that if the colony ever needed the help of a woman it was now. Mr.

Williams is a lumber dealer and was in search of locations for lumber yards. He waited until Seward returned from the homestead. After a short conversation, he promised to have two cars of lumber, our greatest need, diverted to Wilcox siding, if Seward would look after them for him. This was agreed to.

April 19 Raining. Surveyors arrive to lay out the townsite of Wilcox, named in honour of 'Bert' Wilcox, train dispatcher at Moose Jaw.

April 20 Seward's 37th birthday. Rain, snow and sleet. Men put stock back in car for protection—by 5 p.m. snow is six inches deep, turning into a blizzard, and to the delight of everyone the first car of lumber arrives.

April 21 Awoke this morning to find everything under huge drifts of snow, furniture, chickens, and my greatest pride, my new cook stove.

April 22 The lumber having arrived, Seward builds a shed for my cook stove. Three sides and a leaky roof, not much protection from the variable winds and rain.

April 25 Men haul lumber to farm and begin work on our shack 12 × 14 feet. Mrs. Geesen and Mrs. Konieczney arrived.

April 26 Surveyors found it necessary to move 'my kitchen' as the location of one of their corner stakes came underneath the floor.

April 29 Surveyors finish laying out the townsite, and the Village of Wilcox is born. Churn two lbs. of butter, gather eight eggs—our income is improving.

May 2 Cloudy and windy, everything wet. We pack up and move to the farm—two miles. Men drive the loads—I walk. Have dinner, the first meal in our new shack. Begins to rain—keeps it up all day. Will return to siding tomorrow for the tent, buggy and pigs.

May 3 Bake bread for ourselves and the Swedes. Seward and I build the pig pen and put fence around the hay stack.

May 8 Cold and dreary. Commence breaking prairie today. Owing to the lack of horse power, oxen are more generally used, as feed is scarce and oxen can subsist better on grass.

May 9 Cold and snowing—men spent most of the day trying to protect the stock, and later fixed the roof and sides of shack.

May 17 There has descended upon us, like a bolt from a clear sky, the *plague* of pioneers—*mosquitoes*. Never before has anything equalled it. There has been an absence of prairie fires for a number of years causing a heavy growth of old grass, this with the present rains provide ideal conditions for these demons of torture, which cover the horses so completely it is impossible to tell, at a distance, the colour of the animals. We are compelled to keep a continuous smudge for the stock, as for ourselves, we have been compelled to cover the shacks with tar paper, fill all the crevices with mud and wear veils of netting at all hours. They relent somewhat from two to four in the morning and that is the only time we can work the horses in the field. *All our breaking is being done by moonlight.*

May 19 Gloomy, cold morning, get up 3 a.m. Seward and Jim go to Milestone, about 6 a.m. begins to rain, rains hard all the p.m. I am alone all day and do the chores at night. Men get home 7:30 p.m. They sold my eggs for 80 cents, and brought me a butter bowl for 50 cents and 25 cents' worth of muslin.

June 6 Plant first garden—radishes, onions, lettuce, peas, beans, cucumbers, sweet corn, cannas and sweet peas.

June 17 First chickens hatched—hen was set May 27.

June 25 Today our Post Office was established, the first mail bag delivered from the train and Wilcox takes on the dignity of a town. Henry Scheibel has been appointed Postmaster.

June 28 Our first experience with Canadian cutworms—took most of our garden last night.

July 2 Seward goes to Rouleau for load of coal, the horses give out, have to leave the load, on the prairie, will go after it tomorrow. There is no trail. I hang the lantern on the barn to guide him home.

July 3 Rains all night, tent leaks, Seward and I take our bed into the shack.

July 10 Hot day, men work all day building our cave, bake bread for the Swedes.

July 14 Began making hay today. Owing to the absence of fires, the growth of 'Prairie Wool' is heavy and will yield a big crop. We have also solved the problem of what to do with our surplus furniture and piano—which we were foolish enough to bring with us. We put boards in the bottom of one of the stacks, on top of these the furniture and piano, and over all stacked the hay. The stacking was done by a neighbour, 'Otto, the Swede' who claimed to be an expert, a claim he justly deserves, but he built the stack so high, when finished, there was no way for him to get down. We took a 100-foot rope, threw it over the stack, we held one end while

Otto was to take hold of the other and let himself down on the opposite side. We waited for the pull on the rope but it never came. Presently, Otto came staggering around the stack, his face as white as death. When we asked him how he got down, he replied: 'By yiminy, I missed the rope!' Fortunately he landed on a soft pile of hay.

July 26 The first native, Francis Geesen, was born in the store at Wilcox. Our railroad has not seen very active service for many years and it is almost obliterated by grass and weeds, when the wind blows the grass over the rails, the wheels crush it, and makes it impossible to move a freight train. One train has remained at Wilcox all day, today, waiting for the wind to subside.

August 9 Coronation Day—cold and raining. Seward and Jim put legs on a bed spring to be used for Jim's bed.

August 10 Very cold day—Seward shoots four ducks last night, I cook them for our dinner today. A luxury.

August 14 We eat supper out of doors, Seward goes down for our mail, brings me a pair of shoes, a pair of rubber boots, also some soap and meat.

August 16 Very hot day—at one o'clock in the night Seward is taken very sick, Jim rides one of the work horses to Milestone, 15 miles for the Doctor—I hang out the lantern so he won't get lost—the Doctor comes on the morning train, Jim drives him back after dinner.

August 17 Seward still in bed all day.

August 22 The duck season opens tomorrow, Jim goes to town for some shells, Otto comes over, stays all night so they can get an early start in the morning.

August 23 Get up at 2 a.m. and get the men started for the creek. I go back to bed and sleep until 8 a.m. do my chores and Saturday scrubbing. The men get home at 5:30 p.m. with 115 ducks. Otto stays for supper.

August 24 Otto comes over and we pick the ducks, dress them and salt them down for winter.

August 29 Frost ruins what the cutworms left of our garden and flowers.

September 4 Seward hauls a load of old ties from the railroad for fuel.

September 5 Wind blows all last night, and a perfect gale today.

September 6 Wind blows again today—Seward and I cut oats in a.m. and stook in p.m. Men go for load of old ties for fuel—we get bill from the doctor: 12 dollars for one call.

September 18 Our slough goes dry. I take team and two barrels on a stone boat and go three miles for water.

September 23 Otto sends over some apples which I stew and make eight glasses of jelly. In the evening he brings over some potatoes.

September 28 Otto comes over and stays until evening, gets lost going home, and wanders back to our place near midnight.

October 1 Seward begins foundation for our house, the first to be built in the district. It will take a long time as we can only buy the lumber, a little at a time, and Seward and I will have to do all the work, with what help we get from the neighbours. It will not be finished until next year.

October 11 Men finish building the sod chicken house today.

October 20 The well drilling machine, which arrived two days ago, is erected, and the man (Sam Kennedy) begins drilling for water.

November 8 Men build our cow shed, constructed by nailing willows to posts set in the ground, the sides banked to the top with horse manure, and the roof covered with hay.

November 19 Men build a furnace to melt snow for the cows—constructed of sod with a vat—similar to those used to boil maple sugar—on top, and will be heated with old ties as fuel.

November 22 The drill is down 290 feet but no signs of water. I fix up my new chicken house—in readiness for winter.

December 5 27° below. Seward hauls water from Moose Jaw Creek, six miles distant.

December 7 A blizzard rages all day—do the chores and in the evening put paper on the inside of the shack which is constructed of only one thickness of shiplap lumber and the heat from the cook stoves increases the size of the cracks every day; if it keeps on it will soon be all cracks. With the stove and bed there is so little room left we hang the chairs on spikes driven into the beams.

December 24 38° below—the first car of coal arrives at Wilcox—a welcomed Christmas present.

December 25 Our first Christmas in Canada. Seward hauls coal—I make candy in the evening.

1903

January 2 Wash, and churn six lbs. of butter. Hens are laying two eggs a day.

January 12 Nice winter day. Seward and Otto go to Milestone for groceries, I send ten lbs. of butter to trade for our needs.

January 19 The worst blizzard of the season rages. Can't see the barn. Seward goes to milk but fails to return when breakfast is ready. Fearing something may have happened to him, I bundle myself up and start for the cow shed, groping my way. Find the storm has drifted the door shut and he is imprisoned and no way to get out as the walls are frozen solid. I shovel him out and we find our way back to the house.

February 6 Beautiful morning. Seward goes to store for shingle nails, Sorenson comes for a load of lumber, the men shingle some on the house in p.m.

February 11 A blizzard rages all day. I churn four lbs. butter and iron. Seward and Ethan work in the barn making door frames for the house.

February 12 Bright and warm. Seward and Ethan make window frames for the house. About dark the wind raises and a blizzard rages all night.

February 14 45° below, Mr. Sorenson rides the pony to town —pony gets away from him and he had to walk home.

February 21 Seward, Ethan and Otto go to Regina. I wash and do the chores at night, I am alone all night.

February 22 Washington's birthday. Wind changes during night, snow falls and morning brings a blizzard. Wind subsides in the afternoon and nothing but peace and quiet reigns,—a freight passes and leaves another car of coal at Wilcox. Men have not returned. Alone again tonight.

February 23 Chinook wind prevails, I am still alone—men return about 4 p.m.

March 4 One of the Hunt girls was married today—first wedding in Wilcox district.

March 6 Mr. Lundrigan, a new homesteader arrives. Seward does some work on our house.

March 11 Unpleasant day. The house is now enclosed and the roof on, the men move the furniture from the hay stack and store it in the house. I finish my center piece—wash and iron it.

March 16 First car of farm machinery arrives. Seward has the agency for it.

March 28 First spring shower—three antelope arrive and remain several days, one of them came in the yard and played with our calf.

March 30 Another spring day. I rake the yard. Seward goes to Downings for seed oats, gets home after dark, churn three lbs. butter, gather 14 eggs.

March 31 Snow's all gone. Meadow larks are singing. Hawks flying about, crocus in bloom, and the cows drink out of the slough. Men working in the field, the feeling of spring fills the air.

—Mrs. Seward St. John

Prairie summer

The summers were glorious, the creek gurgling through the ravine, the wild roses, the tiger lilies dotting the fields, and when you picked a bunch and held them close to your nose the better to inhale their delightful fragrance, you found your face smudged with the pollen from them, the fruit ripening in the fields —strawberries on the open prairie. You picked hard every spare minute and had a big bowl for supper with real cream and preserved the rest for winter. This happened every day for two or three weeks until not a strawberry was left in our district.

Grasshoppers

Six weeks after their arrival, they attended church with the exception of Mrs. Morrison and baby. It was a beautiful day, clear and bright, but when they were returning home, they noticed a darkening of the sky, but no clouds were visible. When they reached home, Mrs. Morrison met them with anxious looks. 'Did you get wet?' she asked. 'No', replied her husband, 'was there rain here?' 'While lying down with baby I heard rain on the roof or it might have been hail, it sounded so heavy,' was Mrs. Morrison's reply. Just then there was another darkening of the sky, and down fell such a strange shower, the like of which they had never beheld before. Soon everything was covered with a green, hopping, wriggling mess. 'Grasshoppers,' exclaimed Mrs. Graham. 'Now the country is ruined, for they will eat all the crops.' Sure enough, they made great havoc of them and there was very little reaped that season. Such millions of insects floating in the air like a cloud, and when a cloud would come between the sun and them, or a breeze spring up, down they would fall to the earth and devour every green thing in sight. Then they would rise on wings again to fly to new fields, or drop, when the clouds obscured the sun, even if they were over a body of water, as there were heaps of them washed up on the shore of Lake Manitoba.

—*Mary Morrison*

Gophers

Gophers were a dreadful pest in the early days on the prairie, and it was with difficulty that they were prevented from destroying entirely the patches of grain that the settlers had worked so hard to put in. In an effort to rid the country of the destructive little animals, the government paid a bounty of a-cent-a-tail, and every boy and girl in the community was busily engaged in snaring or trapping them. My brothers and sisters took an active part in the campaign, and netted quite a little profit from the business. A number of traps were purchased and placed at various points on the prairie or on the edge of the wheat-patch, and it kept the children busy inspecting the trapline. Each child was allotted the same number of traps, and the competition was keen as to who would have the greatest display of trophies on payday. While waiting to be taken to town, the tails were carefully hoarded and kept in shoe-boxes under the bed.

—*Kate Johnson*

Meadow lark

A prairie fire had burned over these parts the year before and now after the rains the prairies turned green, with the new growth of grass, and how green they were! We often went to the top of a rise nearby which overlooked miles of country. Here in the evenings we would sit for hours and dwell on the beauty of that clean, verdant world. It seemed that a vast, green, rolling ocean, stretching to the distant blue hills had been frozen into immobility. The thought came to me that as the spirit of God had moved over the face of the waters in the beginning of Creation, so might He now move over these untouched plains.

The meadow lark sat near us on a stone, and sang his vesper song. Though I had worked so hard it seemed that he sang to me in my own Swedish tongue 'Nu har du ghordt for lite i dog', 'Now have you done too little today.' The unmerited rebuke seemed to fit his melodic tune, which he sang over and over, until I chased him from his stone.

—*August Dahlman*

Beatrice Benson on homestead, Munson area, Alberta, 1912

Cyclone

There had been a long spell of unusually hot weather, when no rain came to relieve the heat-weary people and parched prairie. One scorching day succeeded the other. On this particular evening, that climaxed an exceedingly sultry day, storm-clouds had hung along the horizon since supper, and by the time the children went to bed, the first, faint flashes of lightning could be seen.

Father hurried through the milking, and then he and mother busied themselves making what preparations they could to protect the baby chicks and other young poultry against the approaching storm. Chicken-coops were moved to more sheltered spots, and doors and windows of out-buildings were closed to keep out the wind and rain. Then, having done what they could, they went indoors. As they were about to retire, two men from a neighbouring settlement appeared at the door, asking shelter for the night, which of course was readily given. While father went with them to put their horses in the stable, mother spread a bed on the kitchen floor, and soon all were settled for the night.

About midnight, my parents, who had been awakened by rumbles of thunder that grew rapidly louder and louder, rose, lit a lamp, and quickly dressed themselves. In a few minutes, they were joined by the strangers who too had risen from their beds. One of these men seemed very ill at ease, and this was readily understood, when he explained that his wife had been instantly killed by lightning during a severe electrical storm just a short time before.

Suddenly the storm that had been so long in gathering broke in all its fury and the rain came down in torrents. Blinding flashes of lightning were followed by deafening crashes of thunder, while a wind of cyclonic proportions rocked the house and threatened to lift it from the ground. Then there came a peculiar sucking sound, followed by the rending of timbers and to the consternation of all the roof of the ready-made house was torn loose and carried away into the night.

Hurriedly, mother and father, assisted by the visitors, carried the terrified children from their now roofless bedroom and crowded them together into a couple of beds that stood in another room. As mother stooped over, tucking in one of the little girls, a flash of lightning accompanied by an ear-splitting crash, lit up the room as bright as day, and the next instant, she staggered as though from a blow. She said afterwards, that she felt as if some one had struck her with a heavy hand across the back, but aside from that she was uninjured. The next morning the little girl was found to have a dark blue bruise on her forehead, while an older child was still in a partially dazed condition, and could remember nothing about the storm, although she had been awake through it all. A shattered pane in the window near the bed over which mother was bending when the lightning struck showed where the bolt had gone through.

The following day, the roof was found across the creek more than half a mile from the house, and with great difficulty it was brought home and replaced.

—*Kate Johnson*

Lightning

In June 1886 Mr. Kline was plowing with one horse when an electrical storm came up and he and the horse were both killed. On the day of the funeral the wheat was about six inches high and it looked like a good crop. Six weeks later you couldn't see a blade of wheat. It had simply dried up and blown away. There were some pioneers who lived on porridge all winter. In 1890, Herbie McLean, our minister's son and Henry Battell were killed by lightning. One man was struck by lightning and killed while milking a cow at 6 a.m., and a woman was killed by lightning while standing beside the stove cooking dinner. Just north of Moose Jaw, a shack was blown across the prairie with a man in it. Such were some of the trials of the early settlers.

—*Grandma Bellamy*

Mrs. C. Bull's home after tornado, McLaughlin, Alberta, c. 1900

Prairie fire

Towards eleven o'clock I was awakened by a painful dig in the ribs and Jack's saying, 'Wake up, Q, the prairie's on fire.' I needed no more poking but dressed as quickly as I had ever done and joined Jack on the back porch where he was emptying sacks of potatoes onto the floor. He gave me one and opened the back door. We immediately smelt smoke.

Jack picked up the two pails of water that we always kept full and ready for use, and went out. The fire was some distance away. 'It always looks nearer than it really is,' someone had told us. I didn't want this one any closer, but what I wanted mattered not to the fire. On it came. We stood and watched it: no sense in going a quarter of a mile to meet it!

The noise it made was peculiar. I had seen houses burning in London, and heard that noise, but this was so different. In London the flames came out of the windows, great tongues of it shot upward from the roofs, and huge black clouds billowed into the sky, while firemen doused adjoining buildings with water, and more horse-drawn fire trucks, bells clanging, came racing to the scene. Here the fire was low-burning, sneaky. Its mordant edge crept rapidly as a snake glides wherever we could see it—for bluffs and little hillocks hid the line of advance here and there, and it made its own noise, a kind of hissing crackling, with a roar of triumph whenever it came upon an extra heavy growth of grass, or a fallen dead tree. The smoke was blue or blue-grey according to the nature of the vegetation burnt.

Jack put a wet sack into my hands.

'Time to get going,' he said, 'come on, old girl, and be careful not to flick any sparks behind you onto the dry grass.'

The fire was advancing at a terrifying rate across the coulee and up our side of it. It was evil personified, remorseless, destructive, a terrible monster, rushing toward us in a wide, all-embracing erratic line, red-tongued, eager. Somewhere at the back of my mind flashed a remembrance of a loving German father who was so determined to protect his sleeping daughter from all dangers that he touched the ground around her with the tip of his lance, and wherever he touched, a fire sprang into obedient life! Funny how long-buried memories stir and rise to the surface at moments like this.

For one moment I stood, paralyzed. Then Jack shouted at me and we went into the fight. Dozens, nay, hundreds of terror-stricken little creatures dashed ahead of the burning line, rushing past us, some charging against us, heedless of where they were going, intent only on escaping the pursuing horror; driven by a fear far greater than that of humans, their natural enemy. The agonizing screams of those caught by the flame were heart-searing. The flood of them rushed on, running, jumping, leaping, hopping—coyotes, gophers, birds, rabbits. Rabbits and gophers were about the best off, as some of the former could dive into warrens if they happened on any, and many gophers found holes into which to dive. The prairie chickens could not fly well, but a few escaped.

Jack and I slapped away persistently but carefully with our wet sacks at the line of flame. But our pigmy efforts were of little avail. The wind changed suddenly, blowing clouds of pungent smoke and red-hot flakes into our faces, scorching skin, parching mouth and throat. Eventually the line of fire was detoured by some breaking, but undiscouraged it romped away around the end absolutely out of our control, hissing and roaring its challenge to other farmers. The river away off would reduce its front considerably, but we wondered where it would end.

Wearily we plodded homeward, now and then slapping our raggedly-burnt sacks at smoking rose-hips that burst with pops, like batteries of miniature howitzers in action. When we got in we drank and drank and drank. Faces, hands, arms, legs and feet hot, shoe soles scorched. We should have had tea to cool us off, but were too tired to make it. All we wanted was to get to bed, which we did as quickly as possible, just after 2:30. We had been out over two hours, but it seemed much longer.

—*Ellen Lively*

Suicide

There was a Dane in our neighbourhood who had taken a homestead and built a log shack. For six months in his first year of residence he disappeared, presumably to get work and make a grubstake to carry him over the winter. He did not mix very freely with the other settlers but as he was not long out from Denmark and had difficulty with his English, we did not expect anything different. He was quiet, sober, and seemed to be fixing things up around his newly-acquired homestead. One day when spring was drawing near, several of us were at a bee on the adjoining quarter section, erecting a log house for a newcomer, when someone suggested we get the old Dane to give us a hand. Nobody had seen him for a week or so. That was nothing unusual, but the fact that he had not turned up at a bee so very close to his own land was. Someone went over and came hurrying back with the look of a man who had seen a ghost. What he had seen, through the small window, was the old man lying stiff on his bunk, a shotgun beside him and most of his face missing.

The old man's dog, his only companion, was lying at the end of the bed and would not permit anyone to so much as set foot inside the door. A man on horseback was sent off posthaste to town and late that afternoon, just as we were hoisting the top logs onto the building, a Mountie arrived. In the sleigh with him were two local doctors, one who was the coroner. The coroner took charge and a panel was soon chosen from among the neighbours attending the bee. The Mountie, at an order from the coroner, drew his revolver and sent the faithful dog after his dead master. We all gathered around the bunk where the ghastly corpse was stretched out and, again under instructions from the coroner, brought in a verdict of accidental death. It surely looked like suicide; it probably was suicide, but, as the coroner wisely put it, to commit suicide is considered, in the eyes of the law, to be a crime and who were we to saddle this poor lonely foreigner with criminal intent when he had paid the last farthing of debt for anything wrong he may have done while living.

—Philip Crampton, Carrot River,
Saskatchewan

Fire

One day late in March I saw black smoke in the west and I knew a fire was coming. It hit my fireguard about midnight and the guard held. It was a wonderful sight, a solid wall of fire as far as one could see. The whole country was a black waste, all except the quarter section of grass that I had saved. Looking at that quarter section of grassland from a distance, it resembled the size of a postage stamp.

—Z.F. Cushing

Ukrainian Family

At first we went through ten years or more of extreme hardships. It was a struggle for existence. Father had to work in a stone quarry during the summer and in winter he cut logs or worked in the sawmill. There was no other way to get cash to buy household necessities. In summer my mother had to look after the farm and family. She looked after the garden and cut our first small crop of grain with a sickle. Many times I led the oxen while my mother held the breaking plow. Willow scrub and stones made breaking the land a slow and difficult job even for a strong man. One day as we were plowing the plow struck a stone and mother was thrown very forcibly a good distance away. As she was lying on the ground my brother and I rushed to her and started to cry. Mother embraced us and asked us not to cry for she was not hurt. We sat there for some time and then mother told us that we should go home. We did, my brother and I drove the oxen and mother limped slowly behind. I remember her limping for several days, but she never complained and told no one about her troubles.

We had no fancy food but mother always made sure that we had milk, homemade bread, wild fruit and plenty of vegetables. Strawberries, raspberries, saskatoons and cranberries could be had for gathering them. We ground corn between two flat stones found on the farm and could get our wheat ground at a small mill ten miles or so distant. During the winter we could get rabbits and partridge and occasionally we had venison. Tasty soup could be made of these. Rabbit pie properly made with good pastry, some vegetables and the right seasoning was a real treat. Our clothing was all homemade, very plain but warm and comfortable.

In spite of our extreme hardship I never heard my parents complain or suggest that anyone should help them. On the contrary they always told us that strong, healthy people do not need help.

—George Dragan

Food

My brother and I were kept busy picking 'buffalo chip' for fuel. We roamed all over. For many summers it was our only fuel. Coal mines were near, and coal plentiful and free for the digging, but Dad hadn't always time to dig or a team to haul it. Buffalo were extinct then and it was really 'cow chip' we gathered, but buffalo chip we called it; 'chip' is the dried manure found all over the prairie.

When the snow came Dad helped a farmer mine his own coal and the farmer hauled our coal as payment. He also worked for a farmer who gave him part of a pig as wages. He worked picking potatoes and received potatoes as payment. He went to the slaughter house and they gave him a number of sheep and beef heads which mother made into head cheese. A farmer whose potatoes froze gave them to Dad to boil up for our chickens. We found that by keeping them frozen and then boiling them up in cold water with the skins on they were quite palatable, so we used them to help out our small supply. Dad had bought a cow and a few chickens and ducks so we weren't starved by any means but money was a thing almost unknown.

We fared well but it was hard on mother, always so tidy, struggling to keep clean and sane in a one-room shack. I have heard her say that many a time she felt like running our for miles and screaming.

Chores

Kids were limited to certain things, sawing the wood, feeding the pigs and taking the swill from the house to the pigs, cleaning up the yard, boys' work. I'm not talking about the girls and the other things they thought you was good enough to do, helping weed the garden and of course as you grew older, you took on heavier responsibilities, such as getting in the cows and milking and helping around the general way. When you weren't in school you could tramp a load of hay in the hay rack and there were lots of odd jobs to be done. But speaking of myself, my parents saw to it that we did our work when we got home from school and when we finished, our time was our own until bedtime, so that I don't think that I have anything to kick at. The only thing I had to kick at is that I got punished when they thought I should, not when I thought.

One thing I detested was when mother felt it was churning day and I had to turn the churn and carry the water to wash the butter and do everything around the darn thing except making the butter—putting it down and taking the water out of it and then carry the buttermilk to the pigs. It was anything but an entertaining afternoon. Watching that old glass in the lid of the churn to see if it was beginning to clear and of course it seemed as if it was never going to. Probably because the cream hadn't been brought up to the proper temperature before it was put into the churn. In the summer there was a lot of butter-making because we used to put down crocks of it for winter use. Sometimes it got a little strong but we got to like the taste of it so that was alright. Killing hogs in the spring of the year was quite a job too. They used to kill half a dozen of them, big heavy fellows and cut them up and salt them and make them for bacon. Scalding them and scraping them and all the rest of it was quite a job, but the only wild meat was game, prairie chicken and partridge, duck. Game birds were always very plentiful. There was another delightful job I think I should mention, a job that the men felt was a little beneath them, and that was pumping the water for the cattle to drink out of the well. Stand there and turn the old handle and turned it and turned it and the more the cattle drank the more you turned it and you hoped the old well would go dry although it never seemed to. Pumping for a hundred or more cattle was a big job and then there was another job. Fill the pails with water when it was washday and that meant extra pails of water. Extra carrying, particularly if you were going to school and spilt some on your legs and they were wet.

—*Edric Lloyd*

Alex Howard turning butterchurn, St. Luke district, near Whitewood, c. 1910

Roundup

When the spring is late and backward, when there are sudden snow flurries and cold winds, and later on when we have many rainy days, I often think of what it would be like on a roundup in such weather. The feeling of a clammy slicker, sodden boots and dampish blankets persists to this day. The weather had to be pretty bad to keep us in, and even camp in the snow or rain was not all that it might be for comfort. What was worse there was nothing to do except to sit around the tents on bed rolls playing poker or spinning yarns. Perhaps I was luckier than most for, after my father's visit to us in '86, I had a splendid tent. On his return to Prince Edward Island he had had it made of a specially heavy canvas by the sail makers in my uncle's ship yards. I usually took a friend in with me in bad weather and there was room for our saddles. Cowpunchers took great care to keep their saddles dry. They used to fold the blanket on top, cross the stirrups over that and tuck their slickers all around and well under so that a night rain would not dampen them.

The first big roundup was held in the spring of '84. The Bar U wagons went south that year, and we met the wagons from Macleod and Pincher Creek. We covered all the country south to below Lethbridge, being out over two months. Emerson was with us, some riders from the Quorn, 'Nigger' John among them. Before this the little roundups we had had were only local affairs, gathering up the cattle on our own range, and it was the same with the southern ranches. As time went on the cattle drifted farther from home and it was necessary to go farther after them. We adopted pretty much the same system as was carried on across the border. Our roundups were community affairs. The different ranches in a district sending representatives, called 'Reps', to ride with wagons of that part, hence I usually rode with the Bar U representing our OH brand. With the Bar U crowd there were about twenty men and at least a hundred horses.

These Reps took six to eight horses of their own, their saddles and bed rolls. Each man had a good slicker as he had to be out in all sorts of weather. Some of us had tents, and most of us had water-proof tarpaulins in which to roll our blankets and to spread under and over us at night. Some even took cork mattresses. This equipment improved with the years. I don't remember much except a bed roll and slicker on that first roundup of '84.

Each Rep paid so much to the cook and wagon, board money really. Though we were independent riders we were under orders from the wagon boss, who was generally the Bar U foreman. When the different wagons met, a range boss was appointed and all wagons were under his orders. We took some steady, well-broke horses and some young uneducated ones to break on the way. There is no better way to train a cow horse than to break him where cattle work is done. Those chosen to go as Reps by their different outfits were men who could ride and rope and who were strong and hardy, for it was no child's play in which they were taking part.

At last, the great day came when we were to join up with 'The Wagon', as it was called, though always there were two and sometimes three, but in camp or on the trail it was 'The Wagon'. We would throw our stuff on a pack horse and set off, or, as we became more civilized and our belongings more numerous, we would pile them into a buckboard and get someone to drive us to the meeting place while we rode, driving our string of ponies before us. Other Reps would be riding in from the different ranches. There would be much talking and joking among the boys while our horses, herded together, were nickering and carrying on as they do while getting acquainted. Now there were only our beds and belongings to be piled in, the canvas stretched over them and lashed tight. There was rough country to cross and nowhere to replace lost articles. The cook would climb up onto the mess wagon seat and the night herder would go to the other. If there was a third, someone was chosen to drive it. The four-horse teams would be harnessed and hooked to the tongues. A whip would crack, a shout go up and with a strain on the tugs, the wheels would be in motion. We were off! Quite a cavalcade we were. The Pilot rode in front, a man who was well up on the country, the trails and the watering places. The wagons would string out behind him; after them the loose saddle horses, herded together by the riders in the rear. It is a coincidence that for years the start was made on a Sunday. When the day's trail was ended, everyone helped to make camp. The tents were pitched and the wagons placed end-to-end. The corral ropes were fixed to the outside wheels of each, ready to be put into instant use. Two coils of heavy inch rope were kept for just this purpose and carried in the wagon to which they were to be attached. These rope corrals were our only means of catching our horses and were very necessary, as the horses were turned loose to graze, but were in

charge of night and day herders termed wranglers.

On that trail, down to as far as the cattle might have drifted, we passed through an absolutely unsettled land, no towns, no farms, no fences, just one big grass-covered range, such grass as we never see now. The buffalo had been gone for some years, and what cattle there were wandered at will from Sheep Creek almost to the border. We followed the old Macleod trail, used by freighters and bull trains. We passed Trollingers stopping place on Mosquito Creek and The Leavings, another such place where Granum now stands; then nothing to Macleod where a few settlers clustered about the post. Here the south wagons joined us and on again we went through vast emptiness to east of where Lethbridge is now built. We went as far as we found cattle and worked back. It might take about a week to get there and two months to return with the cattle we had gathered.

In looking back how I can see it! Hear it! Live it again! A roundup day! From the first call to roll out in the dawn till we stamped out the last coal of our fire and turned in, a little stiff and no-end weary, to sleep the dreamless sleep of youth.

Breakfast at daybreak was eaten in the mess tent, a hot substantial meal of meat, potatoes, bread and jam, with strong black coffee. Our dishes were tin, and we ate sitting around on bed rolls, or on a box if one was handy, or on the ground. Before we were through, the tinkle of a bell told us the night wrangler was near with the saddle horses. One horse was usually belled because it helped to hold them together. This bell, and the approaching hoof beats, was the signal to get our saddles ready and untie our ropes. These hundred head of loose horses, coming in on the run with their manes and tails flying, made a pretty sight. The night herder drove the bunch into the rope corral; the ends of this were sometimes staked or, often, they were held up by some of the men. When the horses were inside, the herder watched the gap while the cowboys, with their coiled ropes, lined up in front of him. We used strong, light, rawhide ropes, more exact on the throw than the coarser hemp ones commonly used today.

Now everything was quiet for a while in order that the horses might not be frightened into stampeding over the ropes. There would be the hiss of a lariat through the air and the loop would drop over a head; that was all the target we had—a head milling around among a hundred others. One had to be careful and very expert. If the horse was well broke, he led out easily, but if he was young and green he put up a fight. Maybe it would take two or

three men on the rope before he was taken out to where the saddle waited. While the roundup was young and we had not been out long enough for the horses to be gentled, there would be quite a little fuss with some of them each morning, especially as we rode our least broken green horses on the morning circle, saving the better educated ones for the more intricate work of cutting out. There were always men along who had made horses their business. Most large outfits employed several just to break their broncs. The Bar U had at different times Jack Crownover, Bowlegged Charlie and Mexican Jack, a giant of a man, six feet two, or three, and weighing over two hundred pounds. He had a clever trick by which he could throw a horse while mounting that would take the conceit completely out of him. 'Nigger' John did this at the Quorn and Billie Metcalf rode broncs for the Waldron.

By the time a couple of throws had missed, or a horse or two proved ornery, all idea of quiet was given up. If our nerves and tempers had not been tried by a wet night, or a cold drizzly dawn, the morning catch up was apt to be an hilarious affair. There would be jokes and much laughter, good-natured jeers and cries of 'Ride him cowboy' or 'Stick him son', for on all probability there would be several bucking contests going on around the camp, contests between man and horse, for there was no whistle blown, no time limit set, no bucking rolls or regulation saddles. It was ride to a finish.

Ernest Cross had a mean gray horse that used to nearly pound the life out of him every time he rode him. I hated to see it, for though Cross had all the pluck in the world and was game to the end, he hadn't the physique to stand the punishment that the brute dealt out. One morning I saw the gray being led out of the corral, and I said to the big nigger who was standing near: 'Look, John, what they have caught for Cross. Don't let him ride that brute. Go take him and give him H---.' So John went and said to Cross, 'You lemme take dat hoss, boss. Maybe I kin make him more gentle for yu.' Cross willingly turned him over—and did John ride him? He raked him fore and aft; he cut him wide open and he gave him quite a different view of life. I don't think that Ernest ever had trouble with him again.

On this roundup morning when the worst kinks were straightened out of our nags, it was time to string out. The other boys would be riding to meet us, their own little circuses over. Now, though two or more wagons worked together, they camped some distance apart, far enough for the herders to keep the horses

Turkey Track Ranch, c. 1914

separate, but we joined up for the range work. When we were all gathered together, the range boss would give us his orders for the day. He would allot portions of the country to different men who, taking several riders with them, would work that part thoroughly, bringing all the cattle they found back to a common centre near the wagon. In this way, the whole country was covered. These were called circle rides and usually two were made in a day. At noon some riders were left in charge of the cattle gathered in the morning, while the others ate lunch and changed horses; then the herders would be relieved to do the same. We ran across numerous scrub bulls as we gathered. These had to be caught and worked on that they might be sold as fat stags in the fall. They were sneaky brutes and it took really good horses to handle them. As the country was cleaned, the wagons with the cattle moved gradually west, sometimes every day to a new site, but always with a thought to wood and water. In certain districts, barrels of water had to be carried with us, also a bit of fuel. The herd grew daily and was watched day and night, for these cattle were wild and hard to hold. The night herders worked in shifts of two to three hours. They caught up fresh mounts when the day wrangler brought the horses in before dark and tied them to the wagon wheel awaiting their time. If it was a wet or stormy night, they would cross the stirrups over the saddles and put their slickers over all. Oh those night shifts! Sometimes in rain or snow, mostly cold, and always uncomfortable! When the cattle were quiet and bedded down nicely, there was not enough action to keep us warm; when they were restless and wanted to break back, or when snow or rain kept them on the move, there was too much hard riding for men already tired; but the shifts were not long and we were young and strong and bed and camp were all the more appreciated for the time we were out. When we reached a point west of where Claresholm now is, the herd was divided according to the north or south brands. The wagons from the west and south, with their cattle, would move out to their own districts and we would take all northern cattle, numbering many thousand, on with us. Sometimes we would meet our Reps from the western wagons, but often they would have to make a separate drive north with what cattle they had gathered.

There were many rivers to cross, some swollen and swift. It was not easy to get the cattle into them and it required patience and skill, especially with calves. These little fellows would break

back and had to be roped and dragged to the water. Men would have to herd the cattle, as they swam with the current, to keep them from milling and turning back to shore. Often the horses would be swimming too.

It was dangerous work for man and beast, but we made it across eventually and very few cattle were lost. Sometimes the newborn calves were carried along in a wagon; the mothers followed bawling after them. Many calves were born on the trail. When they were a few days old they could trot along nicely with the others. At last the Highwood River was reached. I can close my eyes and see them yet plunging into the rivers, swimming with the current, and scrambling out on the opposite bank with wet sleeked-down coats, the mothers frantically searching for their babies. I can hear again the cries of the riders and the bawling of the calves. We threw the herd on the north side and commenced rounding up all the cattle on that range for branding. It was open country there and many cattle had remained during the winter so we not only had the herd just brought in to handle, but others scattered over a good many miles. There were branding corrals built here and there, to which fuel had been hauled and all made ready for us. As the Bar U cattle were the most numerous, they were cut out first from each day's drive, branded and turned loose; then another and another brand would be worked out until all the calves in that bunch had been gone over. We then would move on to another part until all the calves on that range were branded.

After that the cattle were left to graze where they would, until the autumn when they were again rounded up and the beef gathered.

—Memoirs of Frederick W. Ings, rancher,
High River, Alberta

Circle Ranch 'Round-up' camp, near Lethbridge, Alberta, c. 1890

Threshing gang

Managed to strike Johnson's gang Monday, 6th September 1909, and was hired on at $2.50 per day and board. The first afternoon I was pitching in the field. It seemed a very long afternoon's work indeed, and I was pretty tired at the finish, then for two days I drove a team. My work was to load the waggons as the sheaves were pitched up, and then drive up to the separator and pitch off into the feeder. At first I found pitchers much too fast for me and the horses were very slow and lazy. After this I returned to my first job pitching in the field. This seemed very hard work at first, the sheaves were heavy and the waggons were loaded to a great height. I was troubled with a sprained wrist for about a week, but gradually got more used to the work although I was about the slowest pitcher there was. Had indigestion badly at times; so did nearly everybody. In the afternoon Mrs. Warmkee, the wife of the farmer whose grain we were threshing, took me into the house and gave me a dose of physic and afterwards some supper, the first food for 24 hours.

We were a very mixed crew, quite a number of nations being represented. The boss, Johnson, and more than half the gang were Norwegians. Then there were Yankees, Canadians, a Swede, a Dutchman, a Scot and an Englishman, altogether about 20. We dined in a square canvas structure on wheels which was drawn from farm to farm by Cramer's oxen. We worked from about six in the morning until dark. A sleeping caboose was attached to the outfit but the great majority of the English-speaking party preferred to sleep outside of it. We slept in all sorts of places, straw-piles, haystacks, on top of loaded waggons, in stables, and occasionally in a shack. For two or three nights I went home with a Canadian, Jack Cranton, and slept in his shack. For this I was very thankful as the nights were getting cold. About the end of the first week of October the first snow of the season fell. It was on a Sunday afternoon I remember. It came about 4:30 p.m. and in a very short time the whole of scenery in surrounding country was transformed. The storm did not last long but was very fierce.

Next day I returned to work and put in the afternoon. The snow melted during the day and consequently I got my boots very wet. That night was the coldest I ever experienced. Before going to roost I went into the caboose to warm up by the fire.

Nearly all the gang were in there, all those who did not go home of the 'outdoor' crowd had come in with intentions to sleep. There was positively no room for anybody else—I therefore made tracks for a strawpile and scraped out a bed and then covered myself over with straw. Before retiring, however, I hastily took off my boots and socks, dried my feet and put on another pair of socks. While performing this operation, my socks which I had taken off had begun to freeze. It was cold; the thermometer was down to zero. In the morning I found my boots were frozen solid and I could not get my feet in until after breakfast. When I did finally get them on I thought my feet would freeze, but luckily we had a move to make to another farm before commencing work, and I got warm walking.

—*Noel Copping*

Threshing

What a day it was when the machine pulled into the yard with the great powerful engine drawing the high and cumbrous separator. The old horse-power drawn by three teams of horses was never such a sight as this snorting Traction Engine drawing its great red and white trailer, followed by a water-tank. And what a deep mark was left in the earth by the huge engine wheels with their lugs patterning the black soil. Even though the work in the house was pressing everybody came out to witness the arrival of the Machine as it made its way majestically to the first set of stacks and drew in between them cautiously, and what a temptation it was to wait to see the carriers run up and the canvas spread and the great belt beginning to turn and the pitchers climbing up on the stacks from the highest part of the separator, there to wait for the signal to start to throw down the sheaves to the platform below where the two band-cutters stood with their knives to cut the bands.

When the word was given and the great belt began to turn and the white canvas of the carriers slowly revolved, gathering speed every second until the rhythmic sounds settled into a roaring hum, the yellow straw was thrown from the top of the carriers like a cloud of gold smoke that veered and twisted in the wind! When the pile of straw grew so high it had to be removed the 'straw horses' advanced without anyone telling them, one on each side of the straw pile, and by means of the straw rake to which they were hitched one at each end, they drew the pile to one side and turned around and stood at attention until the pile was again high enough to be taken away.

The farmers kept no hours when the crop was being handled and the whistle of the engine tore through the dark dawn every morning when it seemed the room had hardly had time to get dark after we had blown out the lamp. But in a second or two the raucous voice of the alarm clocks repeated the message both upstairs and down that it was time to get up and in a few minutes lights twinkled in the windows and, before there was enough light to see, columns of smoke were rising into the morning air and the business of the day had begun . . . . There was no rest after that first blast from the engine for the fireman, who had been out since three o'clock getting up the steam, would sound a longer blast if the lights did not show in the windows.

The first man up put on the fire in the kitchen stove and put on the kettle full of water and then went out to feed the horses. We prepared all we could the night before and had sliced bacon and peeled the boiled potatoes and had pans of them ready to put in the oven dotted over with pieces of butter and sprinkled with pepper and salt, and soon two frying pans of bacon were sending out their cheerful incense and another pot of eggs was set to cook. Boiled eggs were easier to get ready than fried ones and to have to stop to remove the shell slowed the men up a little, and that was a good thing for they were disposed to eat too quickly.

The table, made as long as the size of the room allowed, was covered with oilcloth and had sugar bowls and cream pitchers at intervals with a cruet stand in the middle, a fine big silver affair with at least five compartments for pepper and salt, mustard, oil and vinegar in glass containers. . . . We sliced bread a loaf at a time and the table had plates of baking powder biscuits and pitchers of syrup and prints of butter.

At noon we often had soup as well as the meat and vegetables, though some of the men were disposed to belittle the value of soup for they said it filled you up but you soon got hungry after it. It did not 'stick to your ribs like meat and potatoes' but I noticed we never had any left over . . . . I loved to see the great platters of hot roast beef beginning to show the pattern, knowing that a further supply was being sliced off in the kitchen, and that big pots of mashed and buttered potatoes and turnips were ready too, to refill the vegetable dishes, and that the oven was full of baked rice pudding well filled with raisins, and that the big white pitchers on the table were full of thick cream, and if the worst came to the worst, that is if they cleaned up everything, we still had the pantry shelves full of pies and a brown crock full of doughnuts.

There was considerable friendly rivalry in the matter of feeding the threshers and there were dark stories told of certain places where they got no raisins in their rice pudding and nothing but skim milk to eat it with and where the pies were made of dried apples . . . . The woman who had nothing ready for the threshers was almost as low in the social scale as 'the woman who had not a yard of flannel in the house when the baby came'.

—*Nellie McClung,* Clearing in the West
pp. 364-368

1621 STEAM THRESHING, MANITOBA   ON THE CANADIAN PACIFIC RAILWAY   WM. NOTMAN & SON, MONTREAL

Portage la Prairie, Manitoba, c. 1887

Threshing

In those days, threshing was done with the old-fashioned horse-power machine, which according to its custom went one day then stood idle the next two owing to some kind of a break-down. While the machine was being repaired, the men and horses that came with it were eating the poor farmer and his wife out of house and home.

With luck one might get rid of the threshers in a week; that is, barring rainy-days and break-down, but this seldom happened. Indeed, by the time binder-twine had been purchased, threshing-bills paid, and men and horses fed, there was little left to reward the farmer for his long hours of toil. If by any chance there was a surplus, most of it went to the Machine Company as payment on the plough or binder.

When preparing for the threshers, father usually butchered a young animal so as to have a plentiful supply of meat on hand. One year, a pig was killed instead, and every bit of the pork was eaten before the men and machine moved on. It was fortunate for mother that she had a large flock of hens so was able to fall back on eggs when the supply of pork ran out, as it did at the last.

Among the settlers in the district were a number of families from Central Europe and these people were not only illiterate but were of a decidedly inferior type. Usually there were several men from this group on the threshing-gang and how their manners annoyed mother! Bowls of stewed dried fruits were set on the table for the men to help themselves, and one day one of these crude fellows siezed a bowl of prunes, emptied the contents into his soup-plate and hastily ate them. Then, picking up the empty dish, he thrust it at mother, at the same time growling out the word 'More'.

Sleeping-cabooses didn't travel with the threshing-outfits as they do nowadays. Instead sleeping-room was supplied by the farmer, each man usually bringing along his own pillow and blankets for a shakedown on the kitchen floor. In our home, the owner of the machine was treated with a little more deference, and in order to provide him with a real bed the children doubled up, four sleeping in the space that previously accommodated only two. But this the youngsters didn't mind in the least; instead it gave them an added thrill.

—Kate Johnson, 1888

Threshing machine

Grain was cut and stooked and when it was dry enough it was stacked waiting for the threshers. The performance around the threshing machine was as crude as anything. There were men to carry the grain on their backs from the threshing machine to the granaries, others were on the straw stack poking the straw back, the dirtiest job of all. You threw the grain on tables and there were band cutters there who cut the bands and then passed it on to the feeder who was the hardest working man on the machine. An hour was about as much as a man could take on one of these big machines. The steam engine was the power of the farming business. Everyone liked to watch the steam engine turn the separator and hear the whistle. The blacker the engineer looked, the more popular he was, and important.

—Edric Lloyd

Pepper mills

We went west from Hanley, where we started to work threshing homesteaders' stacks. The early threshing machines, as I saw them, were utterly devoid of labour-saving attachments. The steam engine was hauled by four horses; so was the separator, which was the farmers' job to move.

A lad stood on each side in front of the cylinder to cut bands and shove the cut sheaf to the centre where the feeder swept it into the cylinder. The straw came out the rear transferred by a carrier and droped on the ground. Here a man and team bucked it away taking some around to the engine to fire the boiler. The separator had a low bagger at waist level, the grain being run into sacks and hoisted into wagons. The bagger man kept track with a peg arrangement.

The Americans snorted in derision at these peppermills as they called them, but it was astonishing how efficiently they could be moved. At the end of each run, each man and team knew what to do. The belt was flipped off and rolled up teams wheeled into place and away went the outfit to another set.

—Ray Coates

(224) SHACKLETON BROS THRASHING OUTFIT 1898
B.273

Cook car

There was to be a cook car to go along with the threshing machine from place to place. Mother agreed to take on the job, and was to be paid the princely sum of seven dollars a day. She ventured out toward the cook car, which consisted of a frame building on steel wheels. The table seated about twenty-eight men. The cook from the previous year had just walked out, and left dirty dishes and a general mess. When mother arrived, she saw the head of a deer sitting on one of the benches, and it was just crawling with maggots and smelling to high heaven. She asked me to take it outside for her, where I buried it. I had just turned six, and mother sent Peg to help me. After the men would go out at night, mother would find her assistant asleep on the bench behind the table. It indeed was a long day even for us kids. Peg was only thirteen then.

The greatest trouble with the cook car job was the continual moving they had to do. Almost every day they had to take all the dishes out of the cupboards, empty the water barrels and place everything on the floor in order to be able to move, because the old car would bounce, jounce and rattle around so much while in motion. The stove would even shift out of its position. Nobody ever had thought of having a rubber-tired cook car those days. For one to have to go through all that parliance of moving and still cook for twenty-six or more super-hungry harvesters was no easy task. The cook car would be moved by four or six horses, depending upon the length of the move.

The very minute the horses were unhooked, mother would have to fly into action, and get everything back in its place so she could start getting a meal begun. The stove would have to be moved back into its place, the chimney erected, a fire built, and the flap doodle started pronto. Chuck wagon races, mother called them, where you were supposed to throw on the stove, and do the half-mile in so many minutes. In spite of where, or how often they moved, the house flies always either were there waiting, or soon arrived. We had no respite from them.

The work was exceptionally hard, but mother seemed happy. The boss never interferred whatsoever. He was kind and considerate. He had a man named Archie Wilson running the outfit and looking after the affairs of the rig. The crew was composed of a group of young fellows, many of them from around Walla Walla, Washington. They were good men for sport and gay times, but there was nothing obnoxious about them.

The crew went to town on Saturday nights, and raised whoopee, but they always were back on the job on Monday morning and with no hangover. Of course, they were mischievous, like the night they stole a Chinaman's ducks, killed and picked them and gave them to mother to cook for them. She cooked them but 'I warned them never to bring me any more of them, because I said I would have to go to jail along with the rest of them if they were caught,' she told us.

There were sixty days of threshing that fall, a fairly long run. The outfit had twelve bundle teams and four spike pitchers. The men at times would throw some of the bundles in crosswise or any old way in the hope of plugging up the forty-eight inch cylinder machine, and getting a rest while it was repaired. There was no such good luck for them though, as all that old steam engine would do was huff, puff and snort just a little louder, and go right on working.

—*Douglas James, At Long Last—Home*

Lunch

By noon everything was ready: cold boiled ham, sliced potatoes, cheese, apple and custard pies, coffee, milk and plain cold water. Wherever we had been to eat I noticed that cold water was always served.

At a hoarse signal from the engine the men stopped whatever they were doing and came to the house. Some washed up at the bench outside where Jack had put bowls and a pail of water—and some didn't. All but one took their caps off, and that one, I was told later, had grabbed a field mouse and cached it under his cap to take it home to his cat. Alive, of course, for cats won't eat dead mice: at least he said his wouldn't.

They came in, most of them with a polite 'ma'am' to which I responded, asking them to sit anywhere at the table and help themselves.

'You must be hungry,' I remarked, 'after such a long morning's work.'

'You can say that ag'en ma'am,' replied the engineer casting an appreciative eye over the table. He promptly helped himself to a potato which he cut up and smothered with mixed sweet pickle. Then he speared a large piece of ham. I caught myself staring, fascinated at the way in which those men could eat so much, so fast. When the pie session came on, each man turned his plate over, picked up a pie, stuck his fork under a cut section, put a finger on top, and skilfully transferred the section to the bottom of his plate.

While appetites were being satisfied and shyness wearing off, talk became brisk, the chief topics being politics. The political situation concerned itself with the building of a farmers' elevator versus the Company Elevator. An elevator built by the farmers of Alberta, maintained and run by them, and to be called the United Farmers of Alberta. Talk became quite animated until the boss put an end to it, calling the men back to work.

'Nice dinner ma'am,' said he. 'Wish I could of et more,' and he followed his men out and back to the grain field.

—*Ellen Lively*

Evenings

Threshing in those days was not begun till after freeze up, so after fall plowing and backsetting were done and winter had set in, one day a horse power outfit pulled into the yard and with all the neighbours coming to help, it was not long before all the little crop was safely in the granary.

After supper, songs as usual enlivened the evening, when someone suggested the gloves. Most of the Canadians had never seen such things, but were anxious to try conclusions with the green Englishmen. These strong, active, hardy lads were no mean antagonists and gave Marshall and me some pretty rough handling, as their idea was to hit, and hit as hard as they knew how.

—*J. Allan Ewens*

Hauling wheat

The winter months were the time for hauling the wheat to market. As we were about 13 miles distant from the nearest grain elevator, hauling the several thousand bushels of wheat was a major problem, especially if the weather was unkind and the temperature dropped very far below zero—as it often did—and the snow trails became heavy with drifting snow. We bagged our wheat in sacks, heavy cotton sacks which cost as much as 30 cents a piece for the heavier brands. At the elevator we dumped the contents of these bags through a kind of hatch into a hopper where the elevator man would weigh it and give a ticket in exchange. This grain cheque could be cashed at the bank or in most of the better stores.

—*Philip Crampton, Qu'Appelle*

Clothes

I am putting away some of my wedding presents that are really not very suitable to our way of living, which is getting simpler all the time. Among our wedding presents were a set of six table napkin rings numbered one to six. Soon after my arrival here I laid the table and put a table napkin and ring before each place, telling Joe and Tom that rings three and four were their rings. Deadly silence followed this announcement, but at least they did put the napkins on their laps. After they had left the table I retrieved the napkins from the floor. They looked as if the men had wiped their feet on them. I put out clean napkins for the next meal and the same thing happened again so I picked them up and put them in their rings and there they have stayed ever since. Now Billie and I are the only ones who have napkins and the rest of the rings are carefully put away. The table cloths are likely to follow suit, tho' I'm not mentioning this to mother. I find that practically everybody out here has white oilcloth on their tables. It saves so much washing and that is a great consideration, especially as Billie and I are not yet very good at the job. I mustn't forget to tell you that we have another machine and it is more successful than the first one was. This one is a round wooden tub affair on four legs with a 'dolly' attached to the lid. When the lid is down and the handle turned the 'dolly' turns first one way and then reverses. This movement is supposed to bring the dirt out of the clothes. Some comes out judging from the colour of the water and a good deal remains behind judging from the colour of the white things! So I think it won't be long before my table, too, is covered with white oilcloth, with a table centre in the middle as a sop to the conventions, and think of the time and labour saved! I do wish I had learned a few more housekeeping accomplishments before I came out here, there are so many things I am absolutely ignorant about, but I did take *one* lesson in ironing before I was married. Mother became anxious about my abysmal ignorance in running a house, and made arrangements for me to take a lesson in laundry work. Like me, mother thought that washing was easy, any-fool-can-do-it attitude, but ironing was another thing! So I went to a school where domestic science was taught and spent three hectic hours learning how to iron and gloss my husband's collars and dress shirt fronts!!!

I bought a glossing iron and treasured it so that I packed it away in my trunk with my trousseau, only to find that my spouse never wears a collar unless he absolutely has to and then he wears soft ones and as far as his dress shirts—they are deep in a trunk with the rest of his evening attire and there they will stay. You will wonder what Billie wears in place of a collar—large silk coloured bandanas—and very nice they look too. He wears a large Stetson hat, navy blue trousers and white (?) shirts and when it's cold he wears a buckskin coat that he got from a Stony Indian. It's beautifully warm and light to wear. Billie has ordered one for me from Peter Bear's Paw with gauntlet gloves to match . . . .'

—*Monica Hopkins, 1909*

Tea

A woman whom we call Miss Smith of London lives with four brothers and has brought all her traditions with her. I went to call and was ushered in and announced by one of the brothers—a small woman with a very prominent nose and teeth rose from a low chair beside an open-grate stove and greeted me in a voice that sounded to me like a fog horn and made me jump and think anxiously of how long I would be expected to stay. However, I soon became accustomed to this booming sound from such a small body and rather enjoyed myself. Charlie and one brother joined us while another brought in a tea table and then the tea tray just as deftly as any butler. And Miss Smith, who is older than the eldest brother, took it all as a matter of course. They invited us to dine and sleep a couple of weeks ago and I quite enjoyed myself. There was a certain excitement about it that is lacking elsewhere for we had to dress for dinner, and one so very seldom wears a low dress that when one does the occasion becomes a remarkable affair. The dinner was very simple, as they keep no cook, but do all the work themselves, and when we rose and swept from the dining room we did not leave the men to enjoy a quiet smoke only, but to wash up. They appeared later looking guiltless of ever having seen a dish towel or a dirty plate.

—*Mrs. Charles Inderwick*

Front room

The front room always got a new coat of whitewash on the log walls at Christmas and everything was scoured as white as sand or soap could make it. The hand-knit lace curtains, brought from Ontario, were washed and starched and stretched on home-made frames, so they would hang straight and reach the floor. Short curtains were considered slightly indecent. The two long widths of rag carpet in bright stripes with orange warp were brought out and laid on the white floor with the good mats, one hooked and one braided. The home-made lounge had a covering of dark maroon canton flannel and was well supplied with patchwork cushions, crazy pattern of silks and satins, and two log cabins, one made of 'stuff' pieces, the other one of prints. There were two bookcases made with spools, painted black and set with shelves and a 'what-not' of five shelves, on which stood china ornaments, a shell box with a green plush pin cushion on the top, apples filled with cloves and cups and saucers (honourably retired from active service because of cracks, or missing handles, but with these defects tactfully concealed in the way they were placed), coloured glass mugs and, on the top, a bouquet of prairie grasses set in a frosted vase, a lace pattern on deep blue.

When the weather got cold the kitchen stove had to be brought into the big room and it was a family grief when this change had to be made. Later when the storm doors and windows were added and a bigger heater bought, a fine big barrel of a stove, with a row of mica windows around its middle through which the coals glowed with all the colours of a sunset. The kitchen stove remained in the kitchen all winter.

But even when the kitchen stove was in the middle of the big room there was a cheerful roominess about it. The woodbox papered with pictures of the Ice Palace in Montreal (*Family Herald Supplement*) when covered with two boards over which a quilt was spread made a nice warm seat and when we got the hanging lamp from Brandon, with a pale pink shade on which a brown deer poised for a leap across a chasm through which a green stream dashed in foam on the rocks, the effect was magical and in the pink light the whitewashed walls were softened into alabaster.

—Nellie McClung, Clearing in the West
pp. 166-167

Summer

White House,
Ebor, Manitoba
July 14th, 1913

My Dear Lizzie,

I got your very kind letter alright and the hair net enclosed. Many thanks for I cannot get any here. I would have to send to Winnipeg for anything I want such as that. I also got the books and the seeds but I did not put the seeds in the ground as I thought it was too late in the season. I am glad I did not as there was a shower of hail here on July 5th that destroyed all the crops. The hail was as large as hen eggs. Almost all our crop is done with the exception of about 20 acres of wheat and 50 of barley. The oat crop will just be for cattle feed.

Here in this country the rent is paid by giving half the crop so it is not as if you had to make up a lot of money. We are all quite well and the men are breaking up the prairie land now.... I have 90 chickens, four turkeys and three ducks. I have got 11 cents all spring for my eggs. Now they are 20 cents and butter is 20 cents per lb. I am selling it in tubs. They are just like the butts at home with a lid on them. They hold about 38 lbs. I have three cows this summer and I am also supplying three farmers here with their butter as they keep no cows.

When I send my butter and eggs to the store they expect it all to be taken in goods. They call it trading here. Money is very scarce. I do not think that farming is very profitable here. This country suits young men to work for farmers. They get such enormous wages which the farmer is unable to pay....

You wished to know what styles were out here. Well there is none that I see. Almost all send for their dresses ready-made to Eaton's in Winnipeg and they have costumes and dresses just the same as at home. As for hats, you could not wear a large one here as the wind is so strong. It is generally toques with a motor veil that is used. Flowers or feathers is never worn here in this country as they would be blown out of a hat....

Write soon and give me all the news. All join with me in sending kind wishes to you. All kind love from your affectionate sister

'Annie'

Mrs. Thomas Howard's living room, St. Luke district, near Whitewood, c. 1910

4
Community

North West Mounted Police

It was some time near the nineties that the government placed detachments of the NWMP here and there in the hills to facilitate and ensure the patrolling of those less accessible parts, and to keep the force in closer touch with the Indians.

When they asked me if I would take one at my place, I gladly consented, and for some years one or two men were stationed there. The log house the police used was close to mine. It was only one large room, but was nicely floored and its walls were covered with gay cretonne. The furniture consisted of bunks, tables, chairs and stove, but it was very comfortable and looked cozy. They took their meals with me and I was paid for their board and that of their horses for which they used my stable. The police horses were of the best, and were always kept up, fed grain and shod. Our cow ponies usually went bare-footed except in the fall of the year when our cut horses were shod behind because it is on its hind feet that a cow horse turns. Our horses were not fed grain except when working and indeed, in those first years, there was no grain available for them at any time; but the hay was strong and the grass so very abundant and nourishing that the horses did well on it and stood hard riding. They were tough, like their riders, and could stand the gaff.

When the Inspector came from Calgary, he arrived in a police wagon, drawn by four horses, driven by a police driver. Everything was very correct! The wagons were two-seated spring wagons of light make, and the horses the best that could be bought, well-groomed and shining. They would dash up the river flat toward the house in great style. We could see them coming a mile off. The Inspector went over everything most thoroughly—their patrol slips, their equipment and their horses. A Mountie was supposed never to let himself slump, to be at all times neat and trim. Uniforms had to be immaculate and though they had a drab tunic for fatigue duty, they always went off on their patrols in proper scarlet. Very gay and bright they looked against the green and dun of the hills. Their horses and horse equipment and arms were also kept in the same state of perfection, saddles were well oiled, and all buckles were shining. This perfection of appearance had a great influence on the Indians. They admired the bright uniforms and the fine horses and were held almost in awe of their unfailing smartness.

—*Memoirs of Frederick W. Ings*

Mounted Police patrol

The Mounted Police had detachments and each detachment had a district. I don't know how many miles they patrolled but the policeman I do remember. If he got a meal at your place or slept there, he had to get the owner of the place or whoever was in charge to sign a paper that he'd been there and had a meal there or slept. My people never charged him. I don't know whether he put in for it to get a little extra cash or whether he didn't, but we were always pleased to see the Mounted Policeman.

—*Edric Lloyd*

Sgt. Frederick Augustus Bagley,
Calgary, 1884

Diary

Fort Walsh—June, 1880

25th On guard for the first time on the Prairie. Arrived at Walsh in the evening and pitched our tents outside the Fort. Had a heavy thunder storm which knocked everything to pieces.

26th Have been digging trenches around the tents and was sworn in, my time to date from the 25th of June.

28th First drill.

July

1st A holiday, had a cricket match and some foot racing. About nine of the boys deserted and were caught.

December

25th Christmas. Had a grand dinner for which we all chip in to pay expenses. Had the barrack room all trimmed with spruce with several heads of animals and rifles, swords and lances all fixed up around in great style.

January, 1881

18th Had a great ball in the large room.

April

16th Great excitement by two of the boys (Corp. Kenny and Gilbert) deserting while out on a ride of which Corp. Kenny had charge, he telling the rest of the boys who were with him that they need not go any further unless they liked as he and Gilbert did not intend to return to the Fort again but were going across the line. The three men then came back, came into the square on the dead run and reported them gone to the Officer. When a party was sent in pursuit of them they caught sight of the deserters about fifteen miles this side of the line and gave chase and all parties ran their horses till they dropped. Corp. Kenny's horse stumbled and threw him. He left the horse lay and took to his legs and got away. They found his horse lying where he fell but could see nothing of him. Gilbert, when he found his horse played out, cut off the road, left his horse behind him and took to his legs. The party returned today, the 18th, with the two horses and all their own played out.

18th Three more of the boys gone for the other side of the lines, don't know how they went unless on foot. They were not missed until Stables this morning. They left sometime through the night. The three men were Bliss, Brown and Shannon. One of the boys was discharged from the Force after serving six months in the guardroom for stealing—his name, C. Rogers. Some of the men are out looking for the Deserters.

19th Walsh was run in the guard room for refusing to drive a team. Two of the boys bought their discharge.

21st One of the boys, McDonald, broke barracks and did not return till he was brought in by an escort. About twenty of the boys left for Battleford this morning.

27th A lot of Indians were into the Fort having a dance.

29th Piapot, one of the Indian chiefs, demanded admittance to the Fort and was refused. He then threw up the treaty flag and papers with threats that we would suffer for it.

May, 1881

6th Another one of the boys deserted, name Blake.

10th Three of the Deserters were tried for taking Government property and got four months, Mills, Wilbur and McDonald.

16th Three more of the Deserters were tried, Morton, Cooper and Convery and got one year and are to go to Macleod as there is a stronger guardroom there. Scott and Thompson only ten months on account of good conduct and will stay here. The invalids all left for Canada, seven of them. Had snow squalls this morning.

20th Two more of the men deserted, Swart and Davis.

23rd One of the prisoners escaped and got clear.

June

Commenced herding.

July

25th Was taken off herding and put on provost guard in charge of the prisoners.

August

2nd Great excitement over some of the boys, thought they had deserted. Caught one fellow named Fuller. Found his blankets outside the Stockade and he somewhere down Town. The other four were in a half breed house down Town gambling.

4th Fuller tried and got six months with hard labour.

8th Were not allowed outside of the Barracks on account of the Indians threating actions so as to be in readiness in case of need.

9th Indians still the same. All of us were ordered to dress in uniform in case we would be needed. Colonel Irvine and

NWMP, Edmonton detachment

Cpt. Cotton with twenty of us rode up to camp. Found the Indians all riding around and firing off their guns. The Colonel gave them a talking to.

10th Still on provost over the prisoners.

11th All hands turned out on full dress parade after which we were all put on fatigue carrying oats out of the bastions so as it could be used in case of need as they expect an attack from Little Pine and his band as they have been kind of cross grained for some time back.

12th Several of us were ordered to saddle our horses and be in readiness at any moment as three or four of the men were up in the Indian camp on duty and they thought the Indians had fired on them but it turned out to be a false report.

13th Every thing seems quiet today but we are not allowed outside of the Fort.

September

8th Was warned this evening about six o'clock to parade in marching order in one hour for the purpose of leaving in the morning to join the escort at Macleod.

9th Left Fort Walsh in the morning.

15th Reached Macleod after camping several days on the road. Found the place in a very dirty condition, had nothing but fatigues.

17th The Marquis (of Lorne) reached here this morning. Was one of the guard of honour to him when he arrived. Then I was put on guard with another one of the boys over the place where he stopped and slept.

19th Taken off guard and sent on the escort across the Line to an American post, Fort Shaw. Reached there on the 27th. Stopped there two days. On the second day he had us paraded and made a speech, after which he left with an American escort for Helena where he was to take the train. A lot of us mounted and went about five miles on the road with him where he shook hands with all of us. We then left for home again, after having a good time and plenty of whiskey.

Fort Macleod — October

5th Reached Macleod after a pretty hard trip having snow or rain nearly every night. We had to scrape the snow or mud away to make our beds down and then turned in just as we were. I only had my boots off twice on the whole trip and that at Shaw.

12th Still at Macleod. Was one of the guard to escort some prisoners who were tried for horse stealing.

14th Snowing and we are still under canvas.

16th Snowing still, about eighteen inches on the level. All the tents have rigged up some kind of a stove. In the one I am in we have a coal oil can for a stove which makes the tent quite comfortable. The Indian they arrested for murdering young Graburn was tried today but got clear. Have been living on chickens and rabbits, ducks and geese ever since we reached here. Two of us go out every day shooting.

19th They turned the horses out when we came here and brought them in today. They look worse than when we came here and a great many of them are dying.

November

24th Some of the boys left for Walsh today leaving ten of us behind to wait for and look after the sick and played out horses and wait till they are able to travel.

25th Major Crozier had a lot of the men turned out last night about twelve o'clock to give the horses some more hay.

26th He tried the same trick last night but it did not work.

27th On fatigue with three others at digging carrots in the garden. Out of the whole day's work we got enough for one meal.

28th We did so well yesterday that they put us on the same thing again today.

December

2nd Left Macleod for Walsh.

9th Reached Walsh about noon. On the trip we travelled along the foot of the Rocky Mountains from Shaw to Macleod.

January, 1882

17th Left Fort Walsh for Macleod and made the head of the mountain.

18th Camped at Peigan Coulee. Pretty cold.

19th Camped at Bull's Head Coulee. Had a frightful snow storm all day. Could hardly see ten yards ahead. One of the wagons broke down.

20th Camped at Chin Coulee. Pretty cold. Nearly all of us are a little frozen.

21st Camped at an old trading fort called Whoop-Up. Slept on a bench sooner than run the risk of getting my blankets lousy.

22nd Started from Whoop-Up this morning. Got about three miles on the road when a wagon broke down again and I and another one of the boys had to go back to Whoop-Up for another wagon and came along all right till we got about half way to Macleod when the horse that I was riding fell and broke his leg and we shot him on the spot. Reached Macleod between three and four o'clock this afternoon. The Indians seem all quiet again although they had the boys surrounded out at the Blackfoot Crossing which made them think they were going to lose their hair but it passed off pretty well after the police took one prisoner which they brought in here and put in the guardroom. My face is pretty sore where it was frozen.

25th We caught two fellows smuggling in whiskey. They had about eighty gallons.

26th The two chaps were tried. They got a fine of two hundred dollars or one year apiece but they paid their fine. They also lost their horses and the rest of their truck.

27th The QMS spilt about fifty gallons of the whiskey as that is the order to have it all spilt, but as there happened to be some snow where he spilt it, the boys soon gathered it up and took it into the kitchen and made punch of it and before night there was hardly a sober man in the Fort.

February
Have been out on several trips.

March, 1882
Have been nearly all month on the Prairie.

April

5th Was to a dance last night. We were all turned out this afternoon to fight fire so as to save some feed for the horses. Had pretty hard work and hot, too. For the last couple of days we have been breaking in some colts to the saddle—they buck like H.

May

24th Had some sports. Fired twenty-one rounds from the nine-pounders as a royal salute. In the evening there was a dance which was pretty well attended by half breeds and whites. Have had pretty good fun in taking stolen horses from the Indians.

June

7th We gave a Ball which was a great success. Had about eight white ladies and the rest breeds. The whites made it seem quite like civilization. We also gave a grand supper.

9th Was out to the Peigan reserve after two Indian prisoners, one of which made his escape from the guardroom last fall. They saw us coming and gave us the slip so we had our trip all for nothing and I came nearly loosing my colt crossing the river.

19th Was ordered out last night to go after some horse thieves which we were lucky enough to catch about daylight and brought them back, horses and all. Have been on several small trips besides.

30th Had another ball last night. Sent a team up to Pincher Creek for some white ladies. With the ladies from Pincher Creek and those around here, made up about fifteen. There was about one hundred and fifty sat down to supper including half breeds and squaws which made quite a crowd.

July

2nd Out on a small trip.

4th The Americans gave a dance down Town but there was only squaws and half breeds there but we had a good time. Kept it up till after day light.

8th Was ordered out last night to go after some fellow. In crossing the river my colt bucked. Lost my hat and got pretty wet but managed to stick on myself. Had to come back and get another horse and started again having to swim the river and got back in the morning all safe but somewhat wet.

18th Was ordered out on the 9th to go on a scouting party after two of the boys who had skipped out from Calgary on the 8th with two Government horses to see whether we could run across them. We could find nothing so we returned and got here this evening. The boys having been caught by another party at the Blackfoot Crossing were brought in here a couple of hours after we did. They were marched up and tried in the evening and each got six years in the penitentiary at Winnipeg for horse stealing.

25th Went on the Bull train and made one trip which was enough for me and quit on the 31st.

—Diary of William Hill Metzler, NWMP,
June 1880-July 1882

Justice

During the early days of settlement the cause of law and order was well served by what was later to be known as the Royal North West Mounted Police but which in the early days were known as the NWMP or Mounties, the members of this most efficient force often acting in the multiple capacities of prosecutor, counsel for the defence, judge, jury, and executioner, which not only tended to the general satisfaction of all concerned but also saved the Department of Justice considerable sums of money that otherwise would have been expended in bringing cases of alleged wrong doing before a duly constituted court. But as settlement increased there seemed to grow up a desire, on the part of some, for a more complicated and formal method of procedure.

And so, when John Doe was accused of the theft of a shot gun from John Roe a strong plea was made by the former to have the case tried in a duly constituted court and before a duly qualified Justice of the Peace, and the accused stoutly refused to be brought before and tried by what he was pleased to characterize as a red coat that didn't know whether Nero of Rome was burned to death with his fiddle or fell in a well.

—John Easton, Moosomin,
Saskatchewan

Court case

Received summons to act on jury at sitting of District Court to be held at Cannington Manor, District Court Judge (later Chief Justice) Whelmore presiding.

On presenting myself for jury service as above, was empannelled on the case of Smith vs Jones. This case which arose out of the alleged shooting of a horse appeared to be one of general interest, and was freely discussed by friends and supporters of both parties before court opened.

According to facts that seemed to be established by this discussion, the horse in question, a small pony, was thought too old and decrepit to be worth wintering, had been turned out to shift for itself, and in the course of its foraging had broken through the fence and was feeding at a stack of hay owned by the defendent. He, being filled with more or less just indignation, shot the pony,

killing it instantly. No objection was taken to this by anyone for two or three months when Smith, learning that shooting a horse was an indictable offence and having some other trivial quarrel with Jones, entered action with a claim for damages. Considerable indignation was expressed at the action of the complainant, popular opinion, as expressed, seeming to consider the act of shooting the horse to have been one of mercy, not entailing any financial loss to the owner as, undoubtedly, it would have died before spring anyway.

So the case was called, jury empannelled, the defendent pleading 'not guilty' though owning up to the act. Witnesses were called and the case went merrily on. The judge in summing up charged strongly for conviction.

On the jury retiring for consultation, Mr. McDiarmid (later MPP) on being chosen foreman said, 'Look here fellows I don't know much about acting on juries but I think I do know justice when I see it. I'm for acquittal. It don't seem fair to me to make Bill liable to fourteen years for shooting a worthless pony that should be dead anyway. That young judge is feeling chesty, and will give the limit, so this is the verdict I think we should hand in. I wrote it out before I came into court:

> We the Jury sitting on the case just heard are of the opinion that according to the evidence submitted, the horse in question came to its death from natural causes, and therefore find the accused, not guilty.'

Mr. McDiarmid in explaining this rather unexpected verdict to his fellow jurymen said that in his opinion a horse that had received a charge of buck-shot in its vitals just naturally had to die.

On the jury filing back into court and returning their verdict his Honour, looking some of the surprise he no doubt felt said, 'Well! this is the first time I have held court in Cannington Manor and it will be the last', and it was.

—John Easton

Detachment of NWMP at Big Bend, N.E. of Waterton Park, c. 1893

Riel rebellion, 1885

That year came the rebellion. I remember my husband coming home from Winnipeg and telling me he had obtained permission to raise a body of men who knew the country and how to look after themselves, to scout ahead of the main body of troops. Having been an officer in the British army, he had all the military experience necessary. All that he had he wished to place at the disposal of the country. Of course I felt he could do no less. I remember him saying to me, 'Have you my uniform? Can you get it out for me?'

Of course I had it in one of the boxes. We found everything except the spike for his helmet, which could never be found. Afterwards I felt glad to think he had not got it. It might have glittered in the sun and attracted a shot! He came home on Good Friday and rode away in his scarlet uniform of those days on Easter Monday to collect his men and go to the front.

How well I remember the anxious days that followed. Our Indians were quiet and friendly but who could tell how long they would remain so? One thing we found—they had accurate news from the front long before we could get any, and it was known and discussed by them. As time went on they got restless and rumours came to us of disaffection. Many a night as we drew our blinds we fancied there were forms lurking behind the woodpile.

An English lad of eighteen was our 'man' and we had him sleep in the living room in case of need. One night we heard blood-curdling yells from him. The Indians were murdering him and our turn had come, we felt sure.

But the poor lad was only having a nightmare, and we were spared.

Another day an old half breed man came to our door selling fish, a most unusual thing. It did not relieve our fears when we heard it was Morriseau, Riel's father-in-law.

As my husband was a marked man with his scouts, it would go hard with us in case of a rising.

My father-in-law, Colonel Boulton, wrote and urged me to take the family and go east until the trouble was over, but Chief Factor McDonald, whose advice I asked, said 'No'. If we went, it would be thought we had some special knowledge and it might precipitate trouble. 'Keep quiet, stay where you are,' he said. I could see reason in this and felt it was my duty to remain where we were. But with six little ones, they were anxious days.

At last the rebellion was over; but my husband was not to return yet. With his scouts he was sent further west to round up and capture some of the rebels—Gabriel Dumont, Poundmaker, Big Bear—and it was almost fall before he returned to us.

How well I remember that day! There was no railroad to Russell then, and they came riding home, Boulton's Scouts, as they had ridden away—a troop of dusty, war-stained men, riding in Indian file, but oh, so happy to be home again, though with some of their number missing. It was a lovely August day. Russell was quite a good-sized village by then. All the children gathered wild flowers and as they rode in they scattered them before the men. It is a wonderful memory!

Later, I remember the little wooden town hall decorated for a banquet with gay Hudson Bay blankets fastened up on the walls and decorated with motifs of hard tack biscuits nailed up to hold them in place, crossed rifles and flags, and the speeches and songs! There were many musicians among the settlers in those days.

Then came the day when I went with my husband to Birtle, the most central place to gather the scouts—and I pinned their medals on our brave men. A gala day, and much rejoicing and banqueting.

—*Augusta Boulton, 1885,*
Russell, Manitoba

Battleford, March 1885

When the Riel Rebellion broke out in 1885, every loyal person in Battleford and surrounding district sought shelter in the NWMP barracks. I remember when crossing the Battle River, sitting on the bottom of the buckboard at the back, that the water came in the buckboard as the river was melting. That was in March 1885. The barracks were situated on the south side of the Saskatchewan River, about a mile east of the new town. At that time it was surrounded by a ten foot stockade made of logs placed side by side on end. There was a bastion on the south-east corner of the stockade. From there one could get a good view. A trench was dug around the inside of the enclosure and bags of sand piled against the stockade with port holes for the men to shoot through, if necessary. A sentinel was in front of the guardroom, which was in the north-west corner of the stockade. There were more men posted outside, quite close, then more farther out. The next men were mounted and went farther out scouting. At a certain hour, the call would start, 'No. 1 all's well' to be taken up by No. 2 until everyone had answered. If by any chance one of them did not answer, the assembly would sound and all of the men go to their appointed places until it was learned why the sentry had not answered. One night there was great excitement as a shot was heard. The Assembly was sounded and all the men turned out. On investigation it was learned that a sentry had stepped into a gopher hole causing his rifle to go off. If it was cold when the men were out at nights the women who were in the barracks for safety would make coffee and take it out to them. The women and children were in some of the barrack rooms and other buildings and the men and older boys in other quarters. There were ten families and between 30 and 40 children in the room we were in.

We often looked over the stockade and watched the Indians looting the houses and stores that had been abandoned when the people had gone into the barracks. Some days the police would fire the cannon at them and that made them seek shelter. One day the Indians set fire to the Hudson's Bay Co. store and were dancing around it when the gunpowder blew up in the cellar, killing some of them. All of the water had to be hauled in barrels in wagons from the spring on the north side of the Battle River. The men had to carry their rifles in case of attack by the Indians.

It was a very impressive sight when the eight men who were killed by the Indians at the fight of Cut Knife Creek, May 2, were buried. The NWMP brass band led the procession, playing the 'Dead March' and 'Nearer my God to Thee' in slow march time. They were buried in the police cemetary on the south bank of the Saskatchewan River, east of the Roman Catholic Church.

—Jessie De Gear

High River, 1885

For a few weeks the settlers all through the West lived in a state of terror. A big Indian reserve lay to the east of us, two more reserves were not far south and there was the chance that at any time they, or scattered bands of unruly young Indian braves from these tribes, might sweep through the country spreading death and destruction.

Scouts patrolled the ridges, ready to set warning watchfires if an enemy approach was seen. Uncle and Charlie volunteered for part of this work. The wagon stood ready, the horses left at night in the stable, harnessed, with bridles hanging from the hames, ready for attaching. Telescope bags were packed and we slept with our clothes on. We were ready to start for Calgary at a moment's notice. What chance would we have with team and wagon that would take at least six or eight hours to cover the distance, against fast-mounted Indian riders? Poor mama must have suffered torment. We children were only pleasurably excited by the continual atmosphere of danger.

We were not allowed to go far from the house or out of hearing distance, but we gathered and discussed places of hiding if it should prove impossible to take flight by wagon. The favourite one to our liking was a thickly wooded spot close to the creek on the far side.

A neighbour whose wife was Indian was our chief source of information. He had regular communication with her people from the Blackfoot Reserve, and we learned that the Indians were kept busy all day feasting on the best food the Government could procure, as the surest way to keep them loyal and satisfied. A hasty railway trip to Winnipeg and eastern cities was arranged for the principal chiefs and they were shown the almost inexhaustible supply of white men. This did much to calm and discourage any would-be aspirations to regain the territory given over to the white race.

—Julia Asher, 1885, High River,
Alberta

Election

Election-time added a little welcome excitement and stir to the otherwise uneventful life of the settlement, and the many meetings of the hotly-contested campaign were well attended by the people of the community.

Votes were canvassed and bought by both sides, the choice of a bottle of whiskey or a dollar bill being the usual inducement offered the voters. Father was courted by representatives of both parties, as it was felt that if his allegiance could be won, his knowledge of the German language would be a valuable aid in soliciting and winning votes throughout the district, as most of the settlers were of German origin.

With this end in view, a young lawyer who had been enlisted in the ranks of one of the political parties pursued father as he returned from town one day, putting forth all the best arguments at his disposal. But they were of no avail, for father's vote, like Scotland's honour, was not to be bought nor sold. When, as a last hope, the young man hinted that the position of Justice of the Peace could be his if he used his influence in the right direction, father lost his patience. In no uncertain terms he replied that there wasn't enough gold in the Bank of England to buy his vote, and his words must have carried conviction, for his pursuer gave up the struggle and hurried back to town.

—*Kate Johnson*

Running for office

We had to work hard: those who had been wavering before were enthusiastic now. They had been whipped into line on fear of the other man being elected. The other side produced a stylograph sheet called the 'Little Joker', our side brought one out called the 'Big Joker'. These sheets contained all sorts of skits and flashes of so-called humour. I started off to canvass outlying electors, covering marvellous distances, getting little sleep till I had covered the whole district. I received great encouragement. One settlement, however, Bresaylor, was decidedly hostile and it comprised a lot of votes. Seeing it was of little use spending much time there I left it to some of my earnest supporters to try and wean away as many as possible. The night before the election I went over the lists and marked off each man as I had sized him up. What a lot of surprises you get on election day! It was open voting (not by ballot) so we knew how each elector had cast his vote. As near as I could figure out, we should have a majority of 42, after giving the other side all doubtfuls.

The election day came at last. I had all my agents and scrutineers at their various polling places, watching for the un-qualified. They headed off quite a number; the others tried to poll a lot of Indians. Some of them could not even say the man's name but wanted to vote for the man with the big beard. Some of the returning officers played low down on me. My opponent's name was Clink; when a man was slow pronouncing my name, before the voter got out the second syllable the returning officer had already marked it down to Clink. At Onion Lake, although the voters were not numerous—about 30 altogether—they were decidedly hostile to me. One of my supporters, an English Roman Catholic, decided to go there and be present on polling day. He was at his wit's end to know how to turn the tide. When the poll opened the first voter, who was for the other side, was foolishly challenged by the scrutineer for the other side; an inspiration came to my friend. He immediately left the poll and went among the waiting voters, all Roman Catholics, and informed them that William, the first voter, had been made to take an oath by the scrutineer and had been made to swear on a Protestant Bible. That trick swung the pendulum the other way; up they went and voted straight for me. At the close of the poll I had a majority in my favor.

The polls closed. From the polls we had results from, it was evident I was elected. The outlying polls could not reduce my majority below 27. My opponent lost his head. He upbraided his own supporters and blamed the Police boys for defeating him. He behaved so badly he lost the little popularity he ever possessed. After the final count was made by the returning officer, I had 180 votes, my opponent 156; there were 74 absentees or aliens that had been on our lists who did not vote.

—*James Clinkskill, merchant, Battleford*
Saskatchewan

Dominion election, Qu'Appelle Valley, November 3, 1904

Sunday

Saturday was bath night, with shoes cleaned and in a row for church next morning, three girls to be completely outfitted in white embroidery petticoats and dresses. I well remember the fuss of getting ready for church at 11 a.m. Barns were cleaned Saturday evening and horses turned to pasture, with the exception of the team that was needed to draw the surrey. Even at that, early rising was necessary as there were yet many chores to be done.

The breakfast itself was quite an item for my mother, with the men to feed, besides my dad and four lively, hungry children. There was no time to wheedle children into eating, your breakfast was put before you, everyone sat down and ate, and I cannot remember any disorder at the table. If you really disliked something, you were exempt from eating it. I stated quite early in life that I disliked oatmeal porridge, so I was never asked to eat it. Once in a while we would have cream of wheat for a change. This I delighted in, but because I liked it was no reason for having it any more often than usual. When it was served I ate it; on oatmeal days I did without. Dishes were washed and put away.

We must all be ready to step into the surrey at 10:15 in order to traverse the three miles to church and arrive on time. I suppose the surrey in comparison with modern cars would be a thing of mirth, but through childhood eyes this conveyance was the very last in elegance. It was two-seated with a great deal of patent leather at different places. After it had stood in the dark shed for a week and the door was opened on Sunday morning to run it out, the patent leather odour that pervaded the place was simply delightful. It had a very high top that could be used either up or down. We used ours up all the time. There were high patent leather fenders over the back wheels, thus protecting the occupants from danger of mud being thrown up into the carriage.

Arriving at church we would find the yard overflowing with people, democrats and horses. As we stepped out of the surrey, we would sort of give each other another last inspection to see that hair bows were in their proper place and shoe laces tied. As we passed through the gate and finally into the church, my sisters would cast fleeting glances at the young swains standing around in their tight pants and high celluloid collars. As for myself, I was still content with the delight I experienced in greeting little girls dressed as replicas of myself in black stockings and shoes, stiff embroidered dresses, and turned-up sailor hats with black velvet ribbons hanging down our backs.

The mothers were mostly dressed in black satin or serge coats, the more daring ones sometimes wearing navy blue. The satin coats were very elaborate indeed, with large collars and lapels heavily embroidered. The rustle of stiff satin and the tremor of ostrich plumes often filled me with awe. Most of the fathers had moustaches, and a few wore beards. Navy blue or black suits and the more dressy ones wore white starched fronts on their shirt. These I think were called dickies. Buttoned and laced boots were the style and on the head was worn a 'Cristy Stiff', this was a very hard felt hat with a high crown and small brim.

The whole atmosphere may appear in this modern age to be austere, but such was not the case. These people were cheerful, friendly, fun-loving and hard working, and although each had come from different backgrounds and different walks of life, yet the heritage of dignity within the church was deeply implanted in each heart. Children instinctively felt that this was God's House and His presence must be respected.

*—Edna Elder, Broadview,
Saskatchewan*

Choir

Our clergyman Mr. Lloyd is a very musical man and every Wednesday he holds a choir practice at his own house. The first hour is devoted to the music for the following Sunday services after which we have secular music, quartettes, trios, duets and solos—all the best music we can muster. He has now formed a 'Musical Union' and we have already 110 names on the list of members. I need scarcely say I have joined and I thoroughly enjoy the practices they are so splendidly conducted. We really have a very fine choir.

The idea is for all the places around such as Battleford, Onion Lake, Bresaylor all to form branches and practise the same music and then have a meeting from time to time of the amassed choirs. The Lloydminster choir has already been invited to Onion Lake in March (36 miles). The whole party to go in sleighs.

*—Alice Rendell, Lloydminster,
Saskatchewan*

Roman Catholic confirmation group, Elm Park, July 1911

Ministers

The community was made up of pioneers largely from eastern Ontario. The majority were Methodist and a number of 'Horner-ites', a sect organized by Ralph Horner from eastern Ontario, a rebel Methodist, under the official title of the Holiness Movement Church. For a number of years they held tent meetings near our school, then they built a church, the only church in the community. The Methodists, throughout the years, held their services in the school, but in about 1908, built a parsonage and had a resident minister, who also served two appointments to the east, known as Wapaha and Primrose.

The Methodist church frowned upon card playing and dancing, the Sabbath was a holy day and attendance at church and Sunday School was taken for granted. The church service for the young was rather dull. For many years we had no church instrument and no choir. The church service usually concluded with a testimony meeting where most of the members gave personal testimony as to their faith in and devotion to Christ. During the week in winter months the weekly prayer meeting was held in neighbours' homes wherein the old Methodist hymns were sung and prayers were offered, led by the pastor or the local preacher. The minister who prepared a written sermon or spoke from a manuscript was looked upon with suspicion and lacking the inspiration of the Holy Spirit. I recall when a minister suggested that the testimony meeting be discontinued, one of my uncles declared that in such an event, he would leave the church. My father took an active interest in the Sunday School and church, it was therefore natural that our lives revolved largely about the school and the church.

I recall Rev. Chancellor Teeter, who preached on occasions. He was an ordained minister, residing in Deloraine. He was bearded and was quite deaf. He used a black metal sounding board, about 6" × 8" in size, which was carried beneath his suit coat. When conversing, he would grip the sounding board between his teeth and bend it slightly, and apparently could hear with comparative ease. These men were followed by summer student ministers from Victoria and Wesley College, in Toronto and Winnipeg.

The student ministers were all single, and served the rural charge consisting usually of three appointments: Bidford on the west and Wapaha and Primrose to the east. It was necessary they establish residence locally — and it so happened that our home was their place of abode. In addition to establishing a residence they acquired a horse and buggy as a means of travel, for which we provided stabling accomodations.

On one occasion it became my duty to drive Sam Bailey, in horse and buggy, to his services, on a first Sunday in his new charge. We left home in the morning in time to arrive at Primrose — about 8 or 10 miles — for an 11:00 o'clock service. After the service we were invited for lunch by a member of the congregation. After lunch we drove to Wapaha, for a 3:00 o'clock service and from there to Bidford for a 7 o'clock service. This trip proved to be an impressive experience for me. While I drove the horse along the prairie trail, Bailey was quoting scripture and rehearsing his sermon, and during the day I dutifully listened to Bailey preach three sermons, each one from the same text given a similar interpretation. Making one sermon do for three appointments was a new and rather disappointing idea to me. I had the childish impression that preachers were inspired, and I didn't think the Lord could be quite so stingy with his sermons.

— O.S. Longman

Church suppers

In time a church was built. The seats were planks laid on logs and later four dozen kitchen chairs which Dad obtained at cost price. Dr. Thurlow Fraser, then minister at Portage la Prairie, opened and dedicated this church in August 1904. The newly organized Ladies' Aid put on concerts and suppers to pay for the chairs and also for bracket lamps. These church concerts and suppers were really something. I have often heard mother tell of how she personally made up a bushel of potatoes into salad and of how she would make as many as 30 lemon pies. The men used to flock in from the outlying lumber camps and a good many landseekers also used to come. For a time these suppers were put on every week and their fame spread so that when landseekers came into the district they would enquire if there was a church supper at McCreary. The fact that the menu at the local boardinghouse consisted chiefly of salt pork no doubt helps explain the success of this enterprise.

— Dorothy Wilson

Old Presbyterian church, minister and choir, Prince Albert, Saskatchewan, c. 1905

Ukrainian church, c. 1910

Confirmation class, Anglican church, Innisfail, Alberta

School

My first school in Manitoba was on the open prairie. It was an oblong frame building some 18 by 20 feet. It was set up on blocks only and had no banking to keep the wind from sweeping under it. Outside was covered with plain siding and inside was just plain lath and plaster. The heating plant was a big box stove that would take a full-length stick of cordwood. It could be heated until red hot but though near the centre of the wide aisle between two rows of desks the big room could never be evenly heated. I had agreed to teach in this school for 40 dollars per month—480 dollars per year. I arrived in January 1893. I found that board and lodging cost me 14 dollars per month, leaving 26 dollars for other expenses and savings to pay college expenses next year. The secretary of the school board went with me the first morning and I found that I was supposed to make fire at eight o'clock and see that the children swept and dusted the school room each day.

In fine weather this was not a great hardship but at 30 or 40 below zero it was no picnic to walk a mile then build a fire in a temperature as cold as it was outside walking about with overcoat and cap on to keep warm until the pupils arrived just before nine o'clock. There were no storm windows or doors and the pupils could not sit near the walls. We had two long benches. We could adjust the heat by moving the benches. The windows rattled in the wind.

—W.J. Sisler

First day

The teacher sat behind a desk of unpainted wood and when he said good morning he smiled at us and asked our names. Bert told him, his and mine too. By this time, I did not know mine.

He told us we could sit together, until he got the classes all arranged. I was too shy to look around at the strange children but I was surprised to know how many children there were. I wondered where they had all come from. There were fifteen or sixteen.

In front of us sat Annie Adams, dressed in a lovely navy blue cashmere dress, with red piping and brass buttons, and she had two long brown braids with a red ribbon braided in them, and a bow on the nape of her neck and one on the end of each braid. Not only that, but had a circular comb in her hair and a red one at that. I felt naked and ashamed with my round shingled head, destitute of ribbons, or any place to put a ribbon. Annie had every piece of equipment a provident child could think of. The frame of her slate was covered with red felt and her slate rag, a piece of white cotton, had a herringboned hem and a heavy glass salt cellar, filled with water, indicated a source of moisture. She even had a pen wiper.

The teacher was finding out what we knew and looking at the books we brought. When he called me to come up to his desk bringing my books I had nothing to bring but a battered old 'Second-part' Ontario Reader and a slate with nothing on its frame. I could tell of no school experiences at all. 'I cannot read,' I confessed miserably.

He smiled at me again and said, 'Never mind that, you'll soon learn.'

'I am nearly ten,' I said, determined to tell all.

'Good!' he said, 'a very good time to begin school; you'll be reading in three months.' I looked at him then and the compact was sealed. I knew I would be reading in three months. I knew my burden of ignorance was going to be lifted.

—Nellie McClung, Clearing in the West
pp. 97-98

129

(1069) BLOOMFIELD SCHOOL, APRIL 20th 1905.

MATHERS
EDMONTON
ALTA.

Horse Hills School, Horse Hills, Alberta

School

The walls were bare, likewise the windows—not a picture, not a blind, not even a plant. Rows of double desks filled the centre of the room. Back of them, and in front of the entrance door, stood a long black iron stove, with a broad front damper that burned full cordwood-length slabs of solid oak from the forests round about. Each cold Monday morning the pupils stood in a circle around it and tried to concentrate on their 'spellings' or timestables, while roasting in front and freezing behind.

In front of the stove along the east wall stood a homemade bench on which sat a water pail and tin cup, out of which the pupils drank. The school yard did not boast a well and John Campbell brought a pailful each morning from his home across the way. Each drop was precious and what was left in the cup, after thirst had been quenched, was carefully returned to the pail. John also acted as janitor. He lit the fire each cold morning, swept the floor occasionally, dusted less occasionally, and all for ten cents a week.

The teacher's desk and her swivel-back chair, which creaked mournfully every time she swivelled, stood on a low platform at the front. The wall behind was covered with shiny black material which served as a blackboard. The desk, a large box-like affair on long legs, had a hinged top which lifted like a lid and when Miss Young did so, it hid her completely, thus affording an excellent opportunity to give the fellow across the aisle a punch in the ribs. Near at hand on the top lay a three-foot tapering pointer which not only indicated the word on the board under discussion but also brought one sharply to attention if thoughts wandered to the playground or the lunch pails while in class. Within the desk lay the treasures confiscated by Miss Young in an unguarded moment, and beside them a large black Bible with red-edged leaves, out of which she read each morning with great emphasis. Beside it was a long black rubber strap which she applied with equal emphasis when she deemed it necessary. The building had a porch smelling of crumbs where the gophers played havoc with the lunches if the tin pails were left on the floor instead of the high shelf along the porch wall built for that purpose.

The day the beginners were given their primers, as the first readers were called, was a red-letter day. They were about six by five inches with a pliable back of shiny brown material. Above the first reading lesson was a picture of a long-tailed rat running for dear life with a ferocious-looking cat with long whiskers close behind, and below these sentences written in a fine Spencerian hand, 'I see a cat. I see a rat. The cat sees the rat. The rat sees the cat. Run rat run.' and a bit further on 'I see a bird. I see a nest. I see a tree. The nest is in the tree. The bird is in the nest.'

Slates and pencils were in use for the most part. The pencils, which were about five inches long, broke if they fell on the floor, but sometimes the red and white striped paper with which they were covered held them together. A rag and a bottle with a quill running through the cork were the cleaning materials used, but if the water froze during the night and the bottle broke, the good old reliable spit was always there and this together with the coat sleeve was the method used by most of the boys.

In front of the school lay an open space too small for anything save the simplest games such as 'London Bridge' and 'The Farmer in the Dell'. The big boys threw horseshoes and the little fellows played tag and everybody wandered the dense forest which ran east to the town line with everything to gladden the heart of a child. There were tall oaks with spreading branches through which the sunlight flickered, birds' nests and squirrels, wild plums and roses all pink and white, chokecherries, hazel nuts and filberts. Two playhouses side by side among the trees were the pride and joy of the beginners. There they kept house with a mother in each. There they placed all their precious bits of broken coloured glass and china.

Each morning if the cows and horses were not in evidence someone rolled under the barbed wire fence of the pasture to gather wildflowers with which to decorate the rooms—daisies, roses, three-flowered avens, gentian and sweet grass.

—*Zella Collins, Miami,*
Manitoba

Ukrainian school

Area of school grounds—one acre. A garden containing seven beds has just been started. The remainder of the land is occupied by the building and playground. No playground apparatus. Two closets in good condition. No house for the teacher. The school building is 22 by 32 feet with a small hall, in good condition but not painted. Box stove, six windows on the east and west walls are supplied with screens. Seating accomodation for 36 pupils. Furnishings—one globe, one set reading tablets, ball-frame, dictionary, five reference books, five library books, teacher's desk and chair and bell. Water brought from neighbour's well. Janitor work done by all the pupils and the teacher. School closed last year, open eight months this year. The course is not related to the life of the community.

—Government report, Manitoba

School teacher

Most of my pupils exhibited at first some form of negligence in their attire. Their feet were encrusted with mud, from the effect of which the skin was cracked and broken in ugly sores. Their hands and feet were innocent of soap and water; their hair uncombed, the scribblers steeped in grease even before they attempted to use them. The flies found their more than natural home on the children's faces and necks.

The dresses the children wore were made of coarse material; wide, gathered skirts of some mottled color, waists of another hue and bright colored shawls on their heads. Flour bags, dyed different colors, were the main sources for dress material for many girls.

Most of the children brought their lunches to school. It consisted of bread and tea or bread and milk. Occasionally a child would bring an egg or some pancakes. Each child carried a bag, made of flour bags, and unwashed since it left the miller's hands. To see my pupils eat was indeed a sad sight. There was no definite time for eating—the children availed themselves of every opportunity.

In the home, the knowledge of all things is, without the slightest hesitation, made accessible to the children. A little child of six told the child of the lady with whom I live the whole process of the mystery of life. Think of the standard of morals such an environment will plant in the minds of the young people! Think of the Canadian citizens such surroundings will produce!

—Canadian school ma'am, 1917,
Ruthenian school, Saskatchewan

Toporoutz and Chernowka schools at Wroxton celebrations, 1914

Picnic

In olden times picnics were quite in order. The word picnic in those days had an altogether different meaning than the same word used today. A picnic was a social 'get together' of the entire community—men, women, children, hired girls and hired men.

In the very early times it was an all day affair, commencing about 10:30 with both dinner and supper served on the grounds. Later it was decided to commence after dinner and in this way there would be just the one meal to prepare. First there had to be a suitable place selected. Men were busy the previous day making rough lumber tables and setting up soft drink and ice cream booths. Soft drinks consisted of home-made lemonade—made the morning of the picnic by a committee appointed for that duty, and raspberry vinegar. This was a red liquid that came in a very tall bottle, to make a drink a small portion was poured into the bottom of a glass and then the glass was filled with cold water. On hot days the lemonade and raspberry vinegar went fast and many times during the day the committee had to get into action and squeeze more lemons.

All ice cream was made in two large freezers. Ice and salt had to be bought and enough cream collected around the district to supply the ice cream demand for the day. Two men and two women were put in charge of this operation, the women to collect the cream and make the custard, the men to take charge of the breaking up of the ice and the turning of the freezers. These freezers were large, heavy, cumbersome and hard to turn, and, as is often the case the turning of them fell to the willing worker.

The only time during the year that we had ice cream was at the picnic, so you may be sure that the day was longingly looked forward to and lovingly remembered for weeks after.

. . .

For many years the Lansdowne picnic was held at our place. The only one I remember of these was the last one. It was the year the middle barn was built and they made a stairway of packages of shingles up to the loft where a dance was held after the picnic. Also there was a broncho buster there that day from Moose Mountain who was slated to put on an act to amuse the crowd.

The horse was brought out with a great flourish and all the children were sternly instructed to stay within the fence to pre-vent accidents, while the adults stood around in eager expectancy. He got the saddle on and the first jump the horse made the rider forced him into a big slough near by and let him flounder around in there a bit. That was all there was to it and everyone was very disappointed as they thought there was going to be some excitement.

I can remember picnics being held at numerous places, but finally the chosen place for many years was Chapmans for Lansdowne and Sexsmiths for Golden Ridge. Everyone went in wagons and brought food, sandwiches, cakes, cookies and salads of all sorts. Linen cloths were spread on the improvised tables, with the district ladies doing the serving with a great deal of chatter and laughing and boasting about their good pies.

I can still hear Mrs. Dayman shouting out to please come and have a piece of her lemon pie! The night before and the morning of the picnic a close watch was kept on the sky by all the children of the community, if a cloud appeared we trembled and if it rained the reign of tragedy in our hearts was even worse.

—*Edna Elder*

Picnic at gymkhana on Roo Dee Ranch, Pincher Creek, May 24, 1899

Baseball

Some of the boys organized a baseball club and after a few workouts decided they had to have a ball diamond. Accordingly after they had chosen a good location they set a date for a bee. I gave them half a day with a team and wagon. Those boys could handle themselves pretty well. Some were Yankee boys and some wore their old uniforms they had used elsewhere. They had a catcher and pitcher they could depend upon and they were anxious to challenge some other teams. While it was too late in the season to do anything about it, they would start practising early next spring and be ready for any tournaments that might take place.

Boxing

I want to tell you about the Munson Sportin' club. That started in about 1911. The English preacher there was a professional boxer. Well, not a professional boxer but he was champion of Queen's College and I believe he was one of the best fighters that I ever seen. I seen him fight several times and he was also a good instructor. He had a lot of young fellows up there that he was training. And I seen him box once with one of the boys there and he says 'Now' he says 'when you hit, hit hard because when I hit I'm gonna hit hard.' He was a real sport you know. He got mixed up, there was another preacher there, I can't think of his name, I didn't see this myself but I heard about it. They put on the gloves and they got pretty rough and they were knocking the dickens out of one another and they had to jump in and stop them. That went on for two or three years. The homesteaders would come way from Hanna and all over. They had a hall there and they would charge ten cents admission and sometimes maybe they would have as high as 100 homesteaders and different people around and they would go out in the audience and they would pick up anybody, say if I come to you and would you put on the gloves for a couple of rounds, well, and then they would get somebody else. They made it dead strangers. When they get in there well, when they start it wouldn't be too bad, and finally one of them would get a swipe in the face, and away they'd go at her, and you'd see one of the best fights you'd ever seen in your life. And maybe they'd have three or four or five bouts like that during a night. Then if there didn't happen to be anybody they could get, there was always the local boys or a boy in the back there. I guess they'd be lightweights, they were very good boxers. They put up a real good exhibition.

1909

Near Virden, c. 1900

Dance

We had been invited to stay to supper and go over to the hall afterwards where there was to be a dance. I can't say that Billie was very enthusiastic but Helene and I were very anxious to go and of course he gave in. It was the first dance that we had been to in this country and we were longing to see what it would be like. It was really good fun but of course quite different from any we had been to before. We arrived at the hall about ten o'clock. Billie disappeared at once and later on I discovered him up in the gallery. It was quite hard to recognize anyone up there for there was such a haze of smoke the faces were quite indistinct; it was his Cheshire cat grin that I managed to pick out in the gloom. In the meantime Helene and I were having the time of our young lives. When we went out into the hall after leaving our hats and coats in the cloak room we found that they had started dancing. The orchestra was comprised of piano and two violins and was quite good. We did not know many people there. We found out afterwards that the elite do not attend the dances and they expressed surprise at our being there!

They can stay away if they want to but they miss a good deal of fun by doing so and anyway I always did prefer the 'hoi poloi'! Helene and I were very amused at the mode of introductions. Streams of young men were dragged up by perspiring MC's: 'Mrs. Hopkins meet Mr. Jones, Miss Cunningham meet Mr. Jones', and we would smile sweetly and the young man would bob his head and another take his place. At first they all seemed too shy to ask us to dance but eventually Helene was flying around the room, simply dazed at the rapidity of the partner. I followed soon after, more sedately as becomes a matron! The quadrilles were what we loved to watch, a 'caller off' directs the dancers and each figure has a different set of rhymes. Towards the end of the dance the tempo gets more rapid and the ladies are simply lifted off their feet and hurled around and around. I still laugh as I think of the expression on Helene's face as she found herself flying around, her feet off the ground as two youths whipped her and another girl around as fast as they possible could. It's simply impossible to be dignified. You just hang on to your partner's neck and pray Heaven he won't let go of you. After our decorous Lancers these dances were simply marvellous and jolly good fun too. I asked to join in but evidently being married and English it was supposed that I wouldn't care for it. Helene being an Australian was not supposed to be so superior!

Between the dances all the females sat on one side of the hall on the narrowest forms I've ever sat on. On the opposite side of the hall the men gathered, when the music started up for the next dance the males dashed across the floor to their favourite partners and the most popular ones had several suitors claiming her for the dance! The supper was served to us in the hall. We all sat in the same way, sheep on one side and goats on the other. The cups were brought around in a wash tub and we all took one, no saucers were provided but the refreshments were ample and delicious, sandwiches and cakes in profusion were passed around. I found myself copying my neighbour and placed an open handkerchief on my lap and simply took a piece of everything that was passed. About 2:30 Billie came and asked in a very martyred tone as to when we proposed to go home. We weren't a bit tired but we still had a long drive ahead so we said we were ready to go any time. Billie hurriedly departed to hitch up the team before we should change our minds. As it was we had almost to drag Helene from the arms of her partner so loath was he to let her go. It was nearly four o'clock before we tumbled into bed, after having spent a really delightful time.

—*Monica Hopkins*

St. Patrick's Day ball, Sunnyslope, Alberta, 1912

Dance

We were allowed to go to dances on Friday night either in town or in the country. Mostly we were accompanied by a responsible person, but many times we were allowed to go in a group or alone with a young man of the district. In either case we usually received stern admonitions from either our landlady or mother as to the decorum of young ladies on dates. I think I should hasten to add here that in those days there was very little drinking of liquor. Girls never drank and boys who did were in disgrace and shunned by nice girls. Drunks in halls were quickly disposed of by the Master of Ceremonies.

Country dances were mostly held in the homes that had at least one large room. Those were the days of large kitchens and many times during the winter they were turned into a hall for a community hoedown! Bea Elder chording on the piano, Johnnie Courtenay and George Elder on the violins with Bob Hooey calling off made a combination that put rhythmic itchiness in your feet and musical chills in your spine!

How the fiddlers stood it I do not know as there was apparently no let up from start to finish. As long as everyone was enjoying themselves the tunes were reeled off. In order to give the 'caller off' a rest an occasional waltz or two-step was worked in, and he always came back as fresh as ever after the slight intermission. The breaking up time came any time after 3 a.m. and one particularly enthusiastic night my brother and myself went directly from the dance to school. Granted we were a bit early (the fire was on when the janitor arrived) but there was no point in going home.

To have danced a square dance, three sets in a small kitchen, with the light from coal-oil lamps bracketed on the wall, the fiddlers perched on the sink, with the 'caller off' standing on a chair, to have been so close that sometimes there was confusion with the set next to you, to have felt the floor shiver under your feet, to have collapsed steaming with heat from recent exertion onto the bench along the wall (while some considerate soul opened the door on its frosty, creaky hinges) and watched your partner's face become slightly indistinct in the white, frosty, smoky haze that enveloped everyone, is a convivial experience that is not reasily erased from the memory.

—*Edna Elder*

Dancing

Save for December and January, which were probably too cold, we had church service once a month that year, on Friday. At one service, held at Buck Smith's, there was a collection taken in a hat and someone had put in a poker chip instead of money. Mr. Smith took it into the other room and returned with a dollar bill in its place. The Presbyterian service was held at a private house instead of at the Stopping Place, probably because the surroundings were more suitable. There was considerable drinking and gambling done at Buck Smith's.

At Christmas time, Buck Smith gave a dance and we went and met some of our other neighbours. On the north side of the river were two families, the Sexsmith family, just across the river from the Stopping Place, and that of Mr. Findlay, three miles north of that on Tongue Creek. These two families, with ours, were the only ones in the neighbourhood with teen-age children for several years.

That first dance was not a success, for it was very cold and the musicians did not come. However, a mouth organ was brought into use, and Uncle's accordion, and I proudly record next day in my diary that I danced four times at my first dance. The next dance was held at New Year and I mention having danced fourteen times. The third and last for the year was on Valentine's Day at Mr. Trollinger's Stopping Place on Mosquito Creek. It was fifteen miles away, but many there came from fifty miles distant and it was a most successful affair. As I mention having danced twenty-six times, there could have been no wallflowers among the girls. There were few ladies and so many cowboys that half-grown girls and even younger ones were in great demand. The dances were mostly oldtime quadrilles, with the changes called off by someone with a good strong voice. An occasional polka or schottische was thrown in and, once in a while, a waltz, but most of those present preferred the quadrilles, which, toward morning, became more like boisterous games set to music than real dancing. The dancing began at eight and lasted till daylight, with an hour off at midnight for refreshments. I recall that we were tired for days after.

—*Julia Asher*

145

Wedding

Perhaps the greatest event of the season was a wedding which, after invitations were sent around, was to take place when the minister arrived on the CPR and who, after waiting considerable time, dropped in with his shaggy nag and buckboard quite unaware at the home where the wedding was to take place.

Much to the satisfaction of the bride-elect she walked away to the shack of the groom-to-be and announced that the minister had come and to get ready. But on learning this he raised himself from his work and exclaimed that 'he had gone off the notion'.

The young lady retraced her steps some little confused and related the decision.

However the young man evidently reconsidered the matter and came walking along dressed in his best. The neighbours were notified and on arriving the ceremony was performed of the first wedding in the vicinity.

Chivaree

It really meant in our time welcoming the couple just married. If they were good natured about the dreadful din going on about them and invited the company in to partake of refreshments all had a wonderful time. But if the folks inside the house blew out the lights and went to bed, that was indeed a mistake because the merrymakers were neighbours bent on having a good time and nothing was going to stop them. Our boss was also a friend. He told us what it was all about as we came from the east in Quebec. So we opened the door wide and shouted to all to come in. As it happened, the boss had made preparations and we had a party and a good time was had by all. 'Nothing like getting off on the right foot,' he said. They left all their wash tubs and noise makers outside, so we could all make enough noise without all them. We made a lot of lifetime friends that night and we had a wonderful time besides. Somebody had brought along fiddles, so we danced till daylight, which came early, as it was early July when we arrived in western Canada. We were married the 30th of June.

—Jennie Nichols

Broken heart

No story would be complete without its romance, not being a novelist I am unable to present to you a spine-tingling story so I will stick close to facts. In 1908, two attractive young ladies moved in as housekeepers for their brother or brothers. Following in the fall a handsome young widow and her two kiddies arrived to take over household duties for her brother. A not so young school teacher came to spend the winter with her parents in a district west of ours. The race was on.

Every single homesteader made the circuit once, myself included. Some made the second trip but they soon found out that they lacked the qualifications and, as always, the two first-noted ladies captured their man. The young English lads paid their attention to the young widow. This narrowed down quickly to two, Wiles and his partner. They got themselves a nice driving outfit and then for over a year they took turn about courting the widow. Finally, Wiles faded out the picture.

One day in 1909 mother was on her way to Clark's and when only a short way from home she noticed a rider and his horse dashing madly across the prairie. It passed a well-boring machine and came racing towards her and within a hundred yards of her, the rider toppled to the ground. Mother ran over and found it was Wiles. He was dead when she got there. After his partner had gone to work, he shaved, took a bath, attired himself in a nice black suit, drank a bottle of carbolic acid, jumped on a horse and raced into Eternity.

—Joseph Heartwell

148

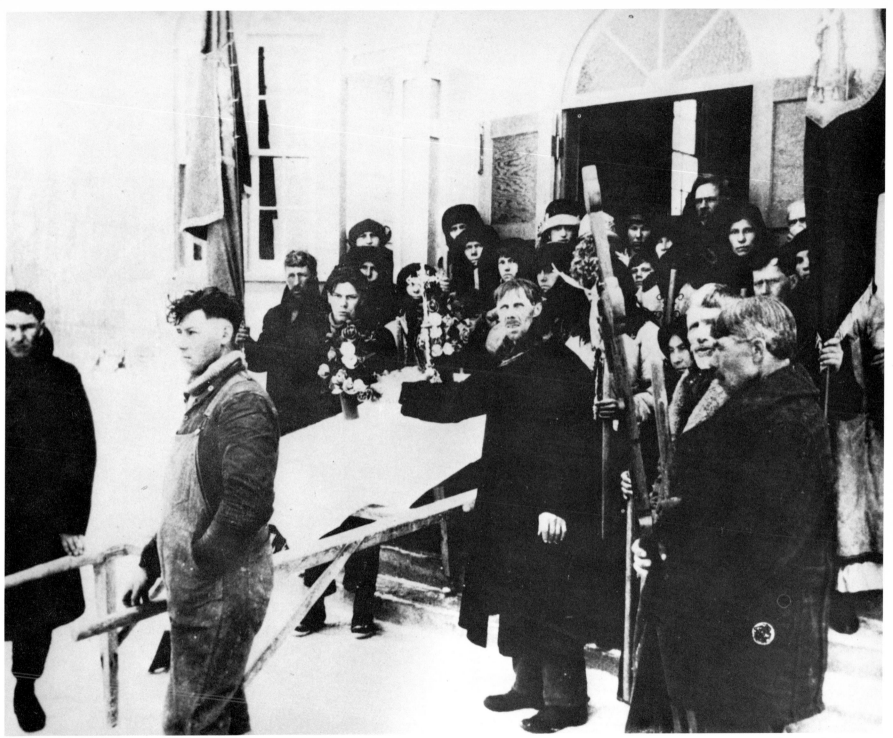

Funeral of Mary Sopwinyk, daughter of John & Tekla Sopwinyk

Church funeral

One of my Dad's first duties was the funeral of a little child. A man and his wife, Swedish people, were passing through to seek work as a chef and assistant in a lumber camp and the child became so dangerously ill that they delayed in McCreary where the little girl died, my mother always thought from diphtheria. There was no doctor for miles and what is more, there was no cemetery. Some of the men in the congregation knocked together a little box which my mother lined with material from her trunk and trimmed with artificial flowers. A piece of land was set aside and consecrated and the little coffin was laid there. The heartbroken parents told how much it meant to them in 'this strange wild land' to have a Christian minister read the burial service for their little daughter.

—*Dorothy Wilson, 1904*

Funeral

The hymn died away, the minister said a prayer, then announced that all who wished to have a look at the remains form a line and do so now. This practice seems to have disappeared through the years, but it was a nice gesture, and although hard to bear, it brought comfort to the family in the signs of emotion that took place at that time.

The pallbearers, (six young men of the district) carried the casket out and placed it in a low boxed sleigh, lined with black robes and drawn by a team of black horses. Wreaths were placed around the coffin. Then the funeral procession got under way to the local cemetery, the minister in the lead with his single horse cutter, followed by the hearse and another sleigh carrying the pallbearers. Then came the family sleigh with the other mourners and a line of teams, sleighs and cutters in which the sympathizing neighbours were riding.

The day was clear and frosty with a bright sun. All that could be heard was the grind of sleigh runners in the snow. Round about lay a vast quietness. None of us said very much, but each was busy with his own thoughts.

—*Edna Elder*

151

Doctor

In 1906 a new doctor came to Saltcoats and soon after referred to me a patient who had moved to Yorkton. His letter of reference was well written and left me somewhat in awe of him as his letterhead showed him to be a Master of Arts and Bachelor of Medicine of Edinburgh University. Dr. S. was an older man than I and had his qualifications some years before I had mine. Moreover, he was imported, and in those days livestock, manufactured goods and doctors imported from Britain were deemed superior . . . .

I saw Dr. S. operate in our hospital on a Saltcoats woman. He seemed more skilful in operating than careful in deciding as to the necessity for the operation. Before closing the wound he asked for a cupful of turpentine which he poured into the abdomen, which in itself was rather indicative of lack of knowledge of the progress made in surgical technique. The patient recovered from her operation but her life was not lengthened nor her invalidism diminished.

Not long afterwards he sent to the hospital a man who 33 years before had been burned from the fold of his groin to five inches below his knee. The burn had been a deep one and the healing process was never complete; the appearance of the granulating surface was suggestive of malignancy. He had decided to have his limb off at the hip and came to the hospital for that purpose.

After a week Dr. S. fixed a date for the operation. He came to do it accompanied by another doctor, a morphia addict, who was to give the anaesthetic. Both were obviously drunk. The patient was too excited to notice the condition of his surgeon and anaesthetist so I interposed, suggesting that we postpone the amputation . . . .He arranged to amputate two weeks later. He came the next time perfectly sober, but he was relying too much on what he had seen done in Edinburgh seventeen years before. He ignored my suggestion to tie the femoral artery until I insisted. That accomplished, he took a long Liston knife and made sweeping cuts, regardless of the hemorrhage. There was a large unnecessary loss of blood, which his assistant had to control almost in spite of him. When he went to disarticulate he floundered. Sticking the point of the knife into the bone about two inches above the socket of the joint he said 'This is the acetabulum,' and broke off the point of the knife.

'Give me that knife,' I said, reaching for it. He gave it to me.

The proceedure at that stage of the operation is to insert the knife back of the great trochanter and slide it up along to the socket of the joint. It was easily done and in a few moments a nurse-in-training stood irresolute with the severed limb in her hands.

—Dr. Patrick

Drunken Doctor

The graduate of Edinburgh soon passed his prime. He mowed a wide swath for a time, for he had personality and training. Deliriously drunk, he often abused his wife. The more delirious he became, the more cruel to her. The town in which he lived felt outraged and some of its citizens acted outrageously. A gang resolved to 'whitecap' him.

One night when he was beating his wife they took him in hand, stripped him, held him over a barrel lying on its side and tanned his hide with apple barrel staves. He complained to the Mounted Police, one of whom went down to investigate. The first man he interviewed told him it was all bosh; the doctor had been having 'snakes in his boots' for a month and that a few days before he had told the local member of parliament of what strange things he had seen. The MP confirmed the statement. The policeman returned and reported that the doctor, in his drunken delirium, imagined he had been assaulted.

Soon the doctor was formally charged with again assaulting his wife. The last time I saw him he was serving a four-month sentence in our local jail, and, as a prisoner, was cleaning up the jail yard.

—Dr. Patrick

152

Residence of Dr. F. J. Goulding, c. 1890

Private Ward, General Hospital, Edmonton, 1902

Appendicitis

One afternoon Dr. Willans from Kitscoty called in to ask if I would go to care for a patient of his ill with appendicitis. On my hesitating he became urgent. It would be impossible to move her even if there were a hospital near. He hadn't operated because he hadn't the necessary instruments for one thing, and there was just a chance that the inflammation might subside. But of course very careful watch must be kept. There was no woman there—in fact they had only one woman neighbour, and she was away in Saskatoon on a visit to a son who had met with an accident in the woods. Mr. Simpson was looking after his wife and putting on fomentations but couldn't carry on much longer without help. The doctor was most urgent in his plea so I said that when Jack came home I would see what he had to say—he had no help on the farm other than mine, but if he could manage for awhile he'd drive me over.

Jack returned about half an hour later, and when he had heard about the Simpsons' trouble, said I'd better go. So I put a few things in my suitcase while he went to hitch up Old Bill, and we were off. It was a long way, but we got there eventually.

The house was small and made of logs but with a lumber roof, set in a grove of trees beside a little lake. Here and there the trees had been cut down and bushes thinned out, giving pleasant glimpses of the water.

As we approached, Mr. Simpson opened the door and came to meet us; a small dark-haired man with a troubled face.

'I can't say how glad I am to see you,' he said. 'If you'll tie up to one of those trees we'll go in,' Jack replied, saying he'd wait outside awhile to rest the horse, then go home.

We entered the house, and went through the kitchen into the bedroom. Both rooms were larger than they seemed to be from the outside, and both had one window giving a view of the lake, and one facing the trail. As we went into the bedroom Tina held out her hand with the wan smile of suffering.

'Thank you so much for coming. With the two of you to look after me I should get well quickly now.'

'I hope so, darling,' her husband replied, taking both her hands in his, gazing down at her with his heart in his eyes. She returned his look with one equally ardent. They were evidently much in love.

I went out to say good-bye to Jack, and watched him until the trail wound out of sight.

It was time for another fomentation and I asked Mr. Simpson if he would like to put it on as he had done it right along. He thereupon turned the bedclothes back carefully, covered the upper part of her body with a folded blanket and went into the kitchen for boiling water which he poured over a folded piece of outing flannel that he'd made into a 'roller towel'. By inserting two sticks he could wring the cloth much tighter and consequently much drier than he could have done by hand.

As the doctor had told me about the fomentations, I had come prepared and was able to supply the one thing needed—a piece of thin white waterproof cloth with which to cover the compress.

After that was done, I went outside, leaving husband and wife together for a few minutes.

The beauty of the calm evening scene struck me, and for a while I forgot everything in the wonder of creation—our tiny earth, the stars which were beginning to show up in an opalescent sky. Birds skimming low over an equally opalescent lake, darting silently, swiftly and accurately at any flies unwise enough to try their luck at an evening's flit above the water.

When I went back indoors Mr. Simpson had put bread, butter, pickles and cold boiled pork on the table. The tea kettle was boiling.

I asked what the doctor had said about nourishment for Mrs. Simpson.

'He said she was to have nothing.' He paused, then went on with obvious hesitation, 'He said he'd try to get here early tomorrow, and bring his instruments in case of need.' Then he burst out passionately, 'I don't believe—' glancing towards the bedroom—'never mind what I believe,' he added more quietly. 'I'll do all I can and only pray that she'll pull through. No thank you, I don't want anything to eat.' No, no, to various suggestions, 'It would only choke me.'

He went back into the bedroom and sat down on the chair by the bed.

Being used to this kind of thing in my district training, I quickly located the dishpan with its accompanying cloth draped over the edge of it, and dish towel on a hook beside the sink. I took water from the kettle, noting the time as I did so, refilled it and put it back on the stove to heat for the next fomentation which wouldn't be due for nearly three hours.

156

Dishes done and put back on the blue and white checkered tablecloth, I went in to suggest that Mr. Simpson should try to get a little rest while I would stay by his wife.

'Yes dearest,' she joined in, 'Do try to get some sleep. You needn't worry now there's someone here.' So he went away and was soon asleep out of sheer weariness and worry, in an old Morris chair by the kitchen range.

She lay quietly for a short time, telling me of little events in her life, how she and Edward had met and so on. When it was time, I changed the fomentation and noted that she was becoming restless. Her temperature was rising, rate of pulse and respiration increasing also.

'Please take off some of these covers, I feel so hot,' she said, then called out 'Oh the pain; please do something.'

Mr. Simpson came in. He had waked up at her first cry. 'She's burning up!' he exclaimed, putting his hand on her forehead and face. 'She's terribly hot.'

'Oh Edward,' she cried, 'I'm in pain and there's something coming away from me. It must be the baby—oh dear! The pain.'

'The what?' I exlaimed, 'you nev—.' But indeed it was, for at that moment an immature child came into the world and caused a complication that had to be dealt with immediately. Of no use to ask why they hadn't told me of it. Obviously the doctor didn't know, or he wouldn't have ordered fomentations unless they were the lesser of two evils. Well I could only concentrate on the exigencies of the moment and try to stop the hemorrhage, and prevent her fainting—she was so exhausted. I prayed that the fever wouldn't take a dive and plunge too low.

The doctor had left some pills for pain and Mr. Simpson went for water and gently raised her head, holding the glass to her lips, after putting the pill on the back of her tongue. When she had swallowed it, and more water in sips, he said, 'There, dearest, you'll feel better now, lie back and try not to worry.'

'Oh but Edward, we were so looking forward to our baby's coming,' and she began to cry.

'I know love, I know. But we can probably have another. Don't cry, dearest, don't cry, please.'

She slowly shook her head and closed her eyes, while he stood looking down at her, holding her hand in one of his and stroking it with the other until I distracted his attention by saying he'd have to get word to the doctor.

'Yes, yes, of course,' he answered, looking about the room as if to find the doctor hiding somewhere in it.

'I'll go across to Jake's and see if he'll ride over and get him, or find him wherever he may be.' With that he took his cap from the bedpost and hurried out into the chilly dawn, by now fast growing into daylight. Jake was feeding his oxen when Mr. Simpson arrived, and as soon as he'd shoved the last forkful of hay into the mangers, he saddled up Dandy Boy and was off at a gallop on his neighbourly mission. I was thankful that the next fomentation wasn't due for a couple of hours and that I'd sent a note to the doctor giving details and asking for instructions.

Mr. Simpson sat by the bed, both of them silent, while I sat on the doorstep—thinking. Suddenly he called out loudly.

'Nurse come quickly; she's getting cold!'

It was true. What I feared, was happening. I hurried to the range and picked up some of the large stones kept there, wrapped them in pieces of flannel hanging over a chair-back and put them to her feet, going back for more which we placed along her sides.

'I feel so cold,' she said, shivering, 'so cold,' she whispered.

'I can't believe it,' said Mr. Simpson, as he stared down at the shaking body, 'Darling don't you feel warmer now?' She could only shake her head slightly and smile feebly.

'What does it mean—so hot and now so cold. What *does* it mean?'

I couldn't give him the awful answer. Her breathing became slower and slower, and finally with a little gasp, ceased —forever. The man looked at me, an agonized question in his eyes, disbelief in his voice. But there was nothing I could say.

'She hasn't gone, has she?' he questioned, 'She can't have—she *can't* have.' And he continued gazing at the still form on the bed.

What can one do in such a case?

I drifted away after having drawn the sheet up to cover her face—and left him alone with his beloved dead.

What can one say at a time such as this when words of comfort fall unheeded on the breaking heart? What does 'life everlasting' mean to the anguished mind? And who *knows* whether there *is* life eternal, and if so, in what form? Who, what, is God?

—*Ellen Lively*

Estevan,
Saskatchewan,
c. 1910

5
Town

Town

Lloydminster is now quite a little town, the rail is up and our station is quite a pretty addition to the town. Little did I think that the whistle of an engine would ever sound so sweet. The passenger service is not properly organized yet as the line is still in the hands of the construction party but as soon as the line is completed and handed over to the CNR company then we shall have a regular service. It is hard for you in the old country surrounded by every comfort and luxury to realize in the smallest degree what we have all put through the past two years in comparative isolation, sometimes without the slightest idea of what was going on in the outside world for a fortnight or three weeks together. For the winter we are comparatively at the mercy of the weather for news or provisions all having to come by road from Saskatoon and when they did come the price of the commonest necessaries was enough to make the pluckiest feel downhearted when we saw the capital we had thought ample to carry us on for a year or so vanishing like dust almost in bare living. 'It will be different when the train is in' became a stock phrase. It was weary waiting and many of us had almost lost heart until one day we heard the rails were laid within two miles of Lloydminster and in less than a week later the first train steamed into Lloydminster. Since then there has been quite a revolution in the price of everything. Flour which we had paid five dols. per 100 lb. bag is now $2.80 top price and everything else in proportion. Lumber too is coming down in price. Town lots have been on the market and bought at high prices. Everyone is now building lumber houses instead of the log shack of the 'old timers'; bricks too are being extensively used for building and this winter will probably be a pretty severe test as to whether they will stand the climate or no. Now three large hotels are in course of erection, stores of all kinds, a fine building for the branch of the Canadian Bank of Commerce, drug store, printing office from which is issued weekly our newsy little paper, the Lloydminster Times. It is just *marvellous*.

—*Alice Rendell*

Town transfer

It was a happy-go-lucky community of young people always ready for a dance or a ball game, until one day the mood suddenly changed when an agent for the railway company appeared and dealt us a low blow as he blandly announced that the village had been built in the wrong place!

It seems that this calamity had been caused by the surveyors, who laid out the townsite more than forty rows of apple trees from the right location. Every building from the large restaurant to the smallest privy had to be moved. Within a day or two a survey party arrived and staked out the new townsite, an exact duplicate of the old one, and the great Lawson town transfer began. A contractor got all the buildings jacked up on long skids. Then all the horses for miles around were hitched to the buildings and drew them by short rushes over the dry slippery grass to their new sites....It turned into a sort of steeplechase with bets made and taken to see who would get settled first. From a distance the moving buildings reminded me of a fleet of small boats sailing slowly across a calm sea.

—*D.E. McIntyre*, Prairie Storekeeper,
p.99

Town of Vermilion under construction, c. 1905

161

Hotel porter

4th November 1909: began work as a porter at the hotel for ten dollars per month and board for the winter. My duties as porter start at 4:30 a.m. when I have to call travellers for the 4:57 a.m. train. I then go to the station, take any mail there is from the hotel, and escort people back from the station, showing them to rooms if they wished to go to bed. Next I clean out and light the kitchen fire, fill the kettles, draw water, grind coffee and set the furnace going by raising a chain and if it needs it, shaking the ashes and putting on more coal. At about 6 o'clock I call Rosie the cook and at 6:30 call Mr. Cattanach's son who waits on table. Then I go along to Newbery's farm for milk, first fetching coal and bread from the cellar and filling the pitcher in the washroom. On returning with the milk I get my breakfast, then I clean out the ashes from under the furnace, fetch vegetables, water, coal and eggs for the kitchen, and if necessary, make an expedition to one of the stores. Then I sweep down the stairs, the hall, the sitting room, the bar and the washroom, dust the chairs and other furniture in the sitting rooms and tidy up generally. In the bar I wipe down the counter every day, change the water in the tank and remove empty bottles to the little storehouse next the hotel. Then I go and clean up, upstairs. After this is finished it is very near dinner time and I fetch more water and coal into the kitchen; then I fill the pitcher in the washroom and have a good clean-up. I next have my dinner while Carl waits on table. When I have finished he sits down and I wait, unless there is a big crowd, when we both wait together. After dinner is over I help carry out the dishes and plates into the kitchen and then brush the crumbs up and sweep the floor in the dining room. In the morning there is always plenty to do, in the afternoon I often have a slack time. I pack empty bottles into barrels in the little house, clean and fill the lamps, fill up the water jugs in the bedrooms and fill the water tub in the kitchen every other day. I have also to fetch in water and coal and get a bit of wood for lighting the fire in the morning. Just before 6 o'clock I go again to Newbery's for milk, then have my supper and afterwards 'wait'. Supper finished I clear and sweep the tables and my day's work is done—between 7 and 8 o'clock usually. During the day the furnace has to be attended to regularly. I have to be prepared to run errands to the stores or the station and carry out slops from the kitchen at all times. Once a week I wash down the stairs, the hall, the sitting room, the bar and the washroom. On Sunday of course there is not so much to do.

—*Noel Copping*

Hotel

At this time there was a generally prevalent fear that all the desirable farms would be taken up if one did not act promptly, so saying farewell to Minnedosa and my brother, I took train for Moosomin, then known as the 'fourth siding', the town consisting of tents and temporary buildings covered with tar paper. A pouring rain was falling, and the first sight to attract my attention was a man carrying a sack of flour vainly seeking some place to put it in out of the wet. Coming to the R.D. McNaughton establishment, at that time located in a tent, the flour bearer asked permission to 'cache' his burden. On being refused he promptly slammed his sack of flour on the floor in the middle of the tent and sat on it saying he would d—d well like to see anyone try to put him out.

During the afternoon of my arrival some enterprising citizen broached some cider that had been shipped in a presumably empty brandy cask, but it was thought later that perhaps the cask had not been properly drained before the cider had been put in, as many of the solid citizens were under the table in a few short hours.

The Royal Hotel was located on the site later occupied by the Queens Hotel, W. Smith, proprietor. Sleeping accommodations consisted of one room that occupied the entire upper story, so the formality of registering was not insisted on. The beds were represented by a pile of blankets in one corner and everyone was his own chamber maid. Among my room mates, about thirty in number, I recall Dr. Rutledge, who was a resident physician in Moosomin, and among others an unidentified person who snored most abominably. All listened wakefully and in silence to the uproar, each believing himself to be a martyr suffering alone, but when the performance was ended abruptly by the performer with a gasp and a snort, and Dr. Rutledge said 'Thank God, he's dead!' a sigh of profound satisfaction was heard from everyone in the room.

—*John Easton*

Edmonton Hotel, 1902-1903

163

Hotel at Hanna, April 15th, 1913

Zimmerman Hotel, Radisson, Saskatchewan

165

Bank

About this date (January 1903) the manager of the Imperial Bank at Rosthern, Mr. Hebblewhite, visited Saskatoon. I knew his father very well, so he called on me and discussed the prospects for opening a branch of his bank at Saskatoon. Of course I pointed out the advantage of getting in on the ground floor in such a promising town. It was arranged between us that I was to let him know if I heard of any move on the part of any other chartered bank coming in. On the train on which he travelled back to Rosthern had arrived a representative of the Bank of Hamilton. I wired him this information. The next morning one of his men came in on the train ready to open a branch of the Imperial. Too late, the Bank of Hamilton had hung out their shingle and started doing business. His man returned to Rosthern by road.

Banker

April 9th, 1882: I am staying at a pretty good hotel for this country. The first night I was here we had no door on the front of the house which made it rather cold. We have not a stick of furniture in our room except the bed. The room is about six-by-eight in size. We have to perform our toilet in a washroom downstairs. Our office is not quite ready, the builders could not get material but we are going in tomorrow to open upstairs in our sitting room and will remain there until the office is ready for use. We have heard nothing of our stationery and books as yet. It is most annoying and has put us to a great deal of expense getting enough to go on with. I have been very busy working from morning until night getting things ready.

April 11th: We have our stoves up and are occupying our rooms. We can't get a bit of wood and have been burning odd bits of lumber. Wood is selling from ten dollars to twelve dollars a load (not a cord). We can get nothing done here even for extravagant prices. We had to pay $3.25 for having our furniture moved from the station. Everything costs 200 per ct. more than in Ontario. The blockade in the post office here is if anything worse than Winnipeg. I tried a dozen times today to get my letters and could not until this evening. The clerks often work all night and are now so pushed that no newspapers have been delivered for nearly a week. My valise has been lying here for four days and I could not get it until I hunted through a dozen baggage cars and walked off with it. Everyone helps himself to his own baggage without reference to the baggage man. Great confusion prevails at the station. Hundreds of immigrants cannot even get shelter. Whole cars of stock have been starved and frozen to death. The reckless destruction of baggage and freight is something appalling. The snow blockade has prevented things from being sent down from Winnipeg and one cannot get the smallest trifles. I could not buy a drop of ink in the place. Could not get coal, oil and numerous other little things. I went up to the school house last night to attend the Easter meeting of the Vestry of the Episcopal Church but it had been put off on account of the illness of some prominent members until Thursday. They are going to build a church at once as we have already quite a large congregation. Over five million feet of lumber is being sent here now from the States and in a few months this place will three times the size it is now. Many people here are sanguine enough to believe that we will soon leave Winnipeg behind but I am not one of the number, though we have some advantages that Winnipeg has not. Property is going up at a tremendous rate. With 10,000 dollars one could make 100,000 dollars inside a year. I hope in time to have a good business here but competition for some time will be very keen.

There is already quite a nice society here, about six families. I have been asked out to several places but just now I have to work from 7 a.m. until 10 p.m. and even then I can't get half through. As I am anxious to know everyone I have to spend a good deal of time making friends. I am glad to say no liquor can be sold here, otherwise this would be as bad a place as Winnipeg, which I am sure is without exception the most depraved place on the Continent. . . .

—*John McCall Wallis*

Northern Bank, c. 1910

Banker

In the fall of 1908 the CPR staged an auction of lots at Outlook in the townsite. The spectators were badly bitten by the investment bug. They fully imagined the town would be a second Chicago and paid fantastic prices for choice corner lots. Two large hotels were built as well as several banks, lumber yards, livery barns, machine agencies, two hardwares, groceries and dry goods, besides real estate, lawyers, jewellers, drug store, restaurants, bakery, and almost every type of business, including three churches. After awhile they found they were 'too big for their pants' and had to make adjustments.

Our American friends were used to prairie conditions and were eager speculators, particularly in land. These spiralling speculations were eventually frowned upon by the financial powers, and our easy-going bank manager was replaced by a frosty-mannered gentleman. The prospective borrower would approach, cap in hand, whereupon the book of revelations would be consulted. Perhaps, as a great concession, one could sign a three months' note at eight per cent.

—Ray Coates

Safe

That same summer the Bank of Hamilton took over the abandoned shack that I had found when I first came. This was a great convenience, as it relieved me of the responsibility of keeping the grain money and the trouble of going to Moose Jaw to the bank. The shack was so small that when a large safe arrived from town on a dray it couldn't be passed through the door and had to be deposited outside temporarily. Like so many temporary dispositions it stayed there for many months in the sun and the rain, in the nighttime as well as the daytime. The staff consisted of a young man named Marlatt, who was not only manager but doubled as accountant, teller and janitor. When a customer came in with a cheque too large to be cashed from the contents of the till, passersby would be intrigued to see the manager-cum-teller rush outside and twirl the combination lock on the safe door, swing it open and go back into the bank with a fat bundle of bank notes.

—D.E. MacIntyre, Prairie Storekeeper,
pp. 63-64

Post office

The establishment of a post office was granted to the settlers in the summer of 1905. I was appointed postmaster and the name Sleipnir was adopted at my suggestion. That same fall I started a grocery business on a small scale in connection with the post office in a log shanty adjoining my dwelling.

The first money parcel for the bank arrived at my post office on a Saturday when the bank was closed. I contacted the bank manager as soon as I could find him after the mail was sorted, requesting him to call for his parcel that same day, as I had no space large enough for it in my small safe and no other receptacle under lock and key. He promised but failed to do so. After the messenger called for it the following Monday I casually enquired about the amount of money that was in the parcel. Eight thousand dollars was the reply. What a risk of leaving such a sum of money on the top of a desk for almost three days unprotected with the exception of a few newspapers covering it to obscure it from instant view.

—*H.J. Halldorson*

Mail

On one occasion I asked a man who was passing with a wagon and a yoke of oxen if he would kindly mail a letter for me. I had written the letter after I saw him coming along the trail. He said he would take it along and showed me a basket full of letters he had gathered up since leaving home. Anyone going to the post office always brought out the mail for all the district and it was passed on and on till it was finally delivered. I have had letters at our house for weeks waiting for the owners to come for them.

Sheho,
Saskatchewan,
c. 1907

Camrose, Alberta, c. 1918

172

Great West Implement Co., Edmonton

Livery stable

A livery stable was an institution. It was a place where people could put up their saddle horses or their teams for the day or overnight or by the week or by the month if they wanted to. They could have all their things sent from the stores to the livery stable.

Most of the stores had one horse and a delivery wagon, high with four wheels and quite a good-sized box and they delivered all those things to the livery stable. You made an appointment with your family or whoever was travelling with you, what time to be at the livery stable and you were supposed to meet there and get away then, but you'd probably meet half a dozen neighbours and if there were no women around the men usually took a bottle of rye or scotch or something out of their pockets and had a drink, but if the ladies were around they usually went into a back stall and let on they were talking about a horse trade or something. The livery horses were always very well kept, beautifully groomed and blanketed and the harnesses were well oiled and the buggys were good. It used to be that you'd hire a livery horse for a dollar an hour. If you were going out for the day it would probably be five dollars for a team.

A good livery man was very careful who he let his horses out to. Some of them, though quiet, wouldn't stand too much nonsense and any horse that had spirit was something that had to be watched and they had what they called weights, that round iron thing with a strap in it, they put on the ground the hooked to the horse's bridle if there was no hitching post to tie it to. And usually around town you didn't want a hitching post because you didn't put a halter on your horse because it didn't look smart enough. So they just bridled them and put a checkline and a weight on them. Doctors used to use the weights on their horses around the hospitals and things.

A livery stable had another function. It was usually a place where you could buy horses or sell them. It was sort of a mart and the average livery man was a pretty good trader, a pretty good judge of horses. It was an institution, people met there and they sat in the office and they talked. The old pot-bellied stove would be heating up the room and the little office and you'd sit on the fellow's bed. It was quite a place.

— *Edric Lloyd*

Prince Albert, Saskatchewan, c. 1900

River Street, Prince Albert, Saskatchewan

Innisfail,
Alberta,
c. 1910

General store

When the prices of wool, butter and eggs had been ascertained and the amounts totalled up, so that she knew how much money she had to spend, mother's shopping-list was brought out, and each article checked off as it was purchased. There was print for dresses for the girls and herself, shirting for the boys and father, flannelette for the children's underwear and skeins of wool for winter stockings. All present were fitted out with cheap, straw hats, the lads at home being remembered too, and of course there were shoes for everyone. Tape, buttons, pins, thread and needles were added to the other purchases, and then the groceries were secured.

Not until all the necessary articles on her list were struck off did mother indulge in luxuries, and even these were carefully selected. Usually they consisted of a pail of jam and a pound of real coffee, the latter being saved for special occasions such as birthdays or an occasional Sunday breakfast. What a treat it was, and how much better it tasted than the burnt-wheat coffee coloured by the addition of a little chicory.

Of course there was candy for the children for no matter how little she had to spend mother always had a treat for them. Each was given one or two of the sweets and the rest were put away until home was reached. Then it was laid out on the table and divided into as many lots as there were members in the family, so that each received the same number.

—Kate Johnson

Storekeeper

I thought that in business customers would choose what goods they wanted and pay for them in cash or else run a charge account. I never realized that farmers would have produce to trade. This problem of produce was always a headache to me. If all the women made Grade A butter and always brought in clean, fresh eggs, it would have eased my burden, but unfortunately many women not only made poor butter, but packaged it in an untidy manner. The good ones used pound moulds and wrapped their butter neatly in waxed butter paper, while the careless ones would make up the butter in rolls of four or five pounds, wrapped in nothing but a dish towel, which they retained. The ground rules for this traffic always seemed unfair to me. No matter whether the butter was good or bad the price was the same to everyone, for any woman would have been insulted if her butter was downgraded. And if I sold it, I was supposed to sell it at the same price I paid for it. Much of it was unsaleable and I packed this kind into butter tubs and shipped it off to soap factories in Winnipeg.

—D.E. MacIntyre, Prairie Storekeeper,
pp. 39-40

Sale

I had written all the wholesalers to ship immediately, as I wanted to open on Saturday and had rashly told everybody that I would. We had no post office as yet and there were no rural telephones so I drove into Moose Jaw on Wednesday and found that most of my orders had been delivered and were in the freight shed. Hurrying back, I hired two teams with wagons and on Thursday we brought out two good loads. . . .

I hired Mrs. Taylor, the widow at the Ottos', whose qualification was that she had once worked for Eaton's in Toronto. She helped me to unpack and arrange the stock. . . . Although I was ignorant about business, I was born with a sense of neatness and order. I wanted to unpack my goods, check them with the invoices, price them and arrange them neatly on the shelves, but I never got a chance.

The word had spread and customers swarmed all over the merchandise, helping me unpack, and picking out what they wanted as they went along. They tried on boots and shoes, sheepskin-lined coats, gloves and mitts and overalls. It was like a fire sale. I would have preferred to be left alone, but they were all so good-natured and eager to help that I could not turn them out. I had little idea what to charge and had to rely on Mrs. Taylor's knowledge of Moose Jaw retail prices or the buyer's honesty. Sometimes I just had to make out a bill of the items without prices and tell the buyer that I would send an account later. They were all honest people and I never lost a cent.

—D.E. MacIntyre, Prairie Storekeeper,
pp. 27-28

Storekeeper

I was about 19 or 20 years, then I thought it was time for me to go in for myself. I had saved up about 800 dollars.

I had a brother-in -law, Mr. Silver, and he had a store in Swift Current. There was the railway going through Neville, about 28 miles. He advised me to go open up there at Neville, Saskatchewan. And so I finally got my brother Ace to rent his farm and go in with me, being that I was an experienced salesman, you know, and knew the gents furnishing business very well, dry goods, that I'd look after that department and I'd give him the tough work; he had the muscles.

We went to Neville and we got a man there by the name of Geisbrecht—mostly Mennonite people lived there—he put up the building for us. I think he charged us about 800 or 1000 dollars. It was quite a big building. It was more like a shell, but it was a big building. I think it was about 60 feet deep and about 40 or 50 feet wide. Had a shed in the back. We had sleeping quarters inside. A little room where we could sleep.

It would be cold you know. I'd get up early in the morning. My brother would get up in the morning and we used to make a fire and warm up the place. And through the night in the winter months we used to keep the heater going with coal and wood, whatever it was.

Business developed right away. We used to get trade all the way from the boundary line. And before that all these farmers used to go to Swift Current, and buy their merchandise there. When we opened up, they'd go to Neville. The farmers used to come down—it used to take them quite a long time to come down—maybe a day, maybe longer than that. Some would come with oxen, some with horses and as a rule, they'd come in about four or five o'clock in the afternoon. They'd come in to the store and they would leave their orders there and the orders would run up quite a bill. There was quite a lot of groceries they would buy for their needs. They wouldn't come in every couple of days, they'd come in every two weeks or so. They'd leave the orders and then they would leave and wash, drink and they had some fun in the poolroom or go to the hotel to the saloon, and in the meantime we would work till about 11 or 12 at night, to have the orders ready for morning. They would come in the morning about 9 or so, and then they would pay the bills for the groceries and leave again.

We did very well. In the old days merchandise was less than half than it is today. I think our business must have been around 80 or 90 thousand a year, which is quite a big business. Of course groceries were the biggest item of business. Not as much profit, but we did a tremendous business on groceries.

The percentage was about the same as it is today, as far as gents furnishings and dry goods. I suppose it would run around 40% markup. Groceries, I don't know. They were less than that. For instance on sugar we wouldn't make more than 10%; flour, we used to get a carload of flour and in two weeks it was gone.

We'd have high holidays and we'd always close up and we'd go to Swift Current mostly. We'd stay there for a couple of days. Most of the trade or farmers knew about our being away, even if we didn't write them. As a rule we used to send them out letters. But they knew and they used to just stay home for these couple of days and just come back when we were in. For instance on a Saturday one time there was high holidays on Saturday and we were away. Saturday was always our busy day and it was in the fall too. But we went and we had the store closed. It was the quietest day the merchants ever had in town. We got back — we were in Shaunavon then—Shaunavon was not very far from Admiral—when we were through we rushed back to Admiral, opened up the store, and I think we did as much business in the evening as we did during the whole day.

The credit was the important thing. A lot of them would go into other stores, or they would do business with us, we'll say. They had enough merchandise and we didn't feel like giving them any more when they didn't pay, so they used to go to someone else, you see and try to get credit there. But we got together — one trusted the other — and I would have it all typed, customers and the amount they owed and how they were paying, and the past due accounts, and therefore that I knew when a customer came in and he mentioned his name, then I'd look it up.

—Harry Buckwold, Admiral,
Saskatchewan

Patrons of Industry

They are just starting up a Patrons of Industry organization here which is gradually spreading all through Canada. Members will get their things—implements, twine, groceries, etc., through them at nearly wholesale prices. The merchants in Moose Jaw are not content with a profit, they literally want everything! For example, a bag of flour on credit is $2.50. If one has cash it would cost $1.90. The same with sugar. And besides the discrimination —one man two miles from me gets 13 lbs. of sugar on his bill but Billy Poulter and I get 12 lbs. of sugar for the same price.

—*George Tuxford, Moose Jaw*

Barber

He stood outside the hotel wondering what to do, when he caught sight of a barber's shop sign across the tracks, almost opposite. So he hopped over and went in. There was one chair with a man in it, and three men awaiting their turns. The barber went on with his work without looking up. Sid waited. Presently the barber removed the cloth from his patron's neck, and with a few brisk strokes with a whisk broom said, as he pocketed the money handed him, 'Next please.' With a glance at the newcomer he added, 'I sure hope you're the last, mister, for I want my supper. I ben going it alone all day, 'n' ain't et since breakfast.' Sid replied that he didn't want a shave but a little information, to which the barber asked, 'Why come to me? I ain't no Information Bureau. Try the hotel over yonder,' and proceeded deftly with his work. 'I tried to get a room there but they're full so's every other place seemingly. I came here because I'm a barber, and thought you might be able to help me, though I don't know how.' The barber stopped his operation and looked the speaker over sharply, then said, 'Wait till I get these here off'n my hands, then I'll lock the door and we'll have a pow-wow.' So the little man waited, and in due time the door was locked, and the barber, whose name was Al, let his visitor into a fairly large room behind the shop. It served as bed-sitting room, and contained a comfortable-looking settee, a rocking chair and an armchair of the type known as 'Morris'. There was also a table and a diminutive heater.

'Get my meals at the 'Eatery' next door,' Al remarked. 'Saves time, 'n' you wouldn't believe how busy I am.' He regarded his visitor for some moments in silence then made a suggestion: 'You say you're a barber. Suppos'n I put you up for the night. You kin git your breakfast next door, same as me, then come right back 'n' start in shavin' them greenhorns as come out on every train. There's only one each day, anyhow. One going east and one west. Lordy, what advertising don' do! Well I s'pose the country's big enough. What say?'

'I—I hardly know what to say,' replied the other, 'except that I'd like to try it if it won't put you out. You don't know me—by the way my name's Sid Hollingsworth. You don't know my work, or ——.'

'That's my funeral,' Al interrupted. 'You c'n doss down on that thar couch right now and don't worry about nothing!' He went to a closet and produced two Indian blankets, one of which he threw into the Morris chair, the other on to the couch for Sid. 'Sentry box's out back along with others,' he laughed, as he pulled out the footrest form under his chair and prepared for night by shedding his daywear and donning an old-fashioned night-shirt. 'One of my old Dad's and good stuff too—they don't make it like this nowadays,' saying which he sat down in his chair, putting his feet up on the extension, and was asleep almost at once.

—*Ellen Lively*

Virden,
c. 1900

Chinese

I was born in a village in the province of Kwan Tu in the southern part of China. My father won a military title from the government through the examination. Because of his good nature and his title he gained respect from the people of our village. He received no pay from the country. He operated a store in order to support my family including my mother, two brothers and four sisters. Living with him in the store the accommodation was fine. I had a big piggy bank with lots of coins but never spent one of them. I began to realize my father's situation. At my age of 13 after seven years of schooling I had my father's consent to leave home for Singapore with the ambition to help my father. I worked in a store. My wages were four dollars a month for the first year. During seven years I sent money to my father and still saved some to go back home. I returned from Singapore and got married. Then I went to Hong Kong. Three years were spent in Hong Kong.

I landed in Canada for the first time in 1913 and my age was 25. I paid 200 dollars for my boat ticket and 500 dollars head tax. My father sold a piece of land. I stayed on the west coast for a short while and then came to Saskatchewan. For 30 years in the restaurant business I was around Aneroid, Cadillac, Consul, Vanguard, Hazelmore, Willow Bunch, Arcola, Somme and Assiniboia. The longest period was spent in Somme. Somme was a new town surrounded by plenty of bush inhabited by only a handful of people and business was in general poor. I had to stay there ten years before I had a chance to go out. I remember the first day I came I sold only a piece of pie at noon and a chocolate bar the next day at 10 in the evening just before closing time, also for five cents a piece. Bread and potatoes were my only food, hard wood my bed and rain and snow my drinking water. In very cold days the water in the rear part of the store froze.

I was all alone. I baked my pies, cakes and made the ice cream in summer, washed the dishes and waited on the tables. The building was 12 by 30 and about eight feet high. The front part was about 12 by 20 and then there was the part at the back where I baked, washed the dishes and slept beside a wood burning stove. I did not have a bed but made a double-decker bunk with neither spring nor mattress. I usually slept in the lowest bunk but when I had guests I took the upper and left the lower for company.

I made my first trip back to China in 1918. I stayed one year, when my daughter was born. I went for my second visit in 1924. The Canadian immigration would not permit me to stay more than two years so my boy was born shortly after I returned to Canada. Although he lived to be 14 I never saw him.

—*Charlie Kwan*

Interpreter

Charlie Yuen came to San Francisco from China when he was nearly thirteen years old. He lived with an uncle in San Francisco who was to teach him his business and who tried to send him to school. Charlie only attended for half a day and refused to return; as a result, he could neither read nor write. He was, however, blessed with a wonderful memory and in later years he was noted for his facility to remember telephone numbers and messages.

Charlie made his way to British Columbia in 1881. At the time of the construction of the Canadian Pacific Railway, he was in charge of a group of Chinese workers. He acted as foreman, and during the laying of track in the Kicking Horse Pass he met Johnny Hamilton, who was driving a stage coach.

W.R. Hull brought Charlie to Alberta to assist in irrigation, and when Mr. Hull bought the Bow Valley Farm, around 1891, Charlie was installed as cook and general handyman, doing anything from butchering a steer to ironing out problems.

Charlie Yuen was over six feet tall and dressed extremely well. During his early years in Canada he wore his hair in a pigtail, as he would not have been permitted to return to China if he had cut it off. On one of his trips, Charlie married and in due course a son was born; however, according to the custom of the times, his wife and child remained in China while Charlie supported them, returning on one or two occasions. A daughter was also born later.

Charlie returned to China in 1938 to the town of Hai Ping about 200 miles north of Canton, hoping to end his days peacefully there. However, he failed to locate his family who had been scattered by the troublous times in China, and it is said he died of a broken heart.

—*Georgeen Barrass, from an interview with Mr. and Mrs. E.F. Hoschka, Calgary*

Lem's restaurant, High River

Fire

Saturday, 14th November. I went up to my room early for the purpose of having a good wash. While engaged in my ablutions Mr. Cattanach came knocking at my door telling me to get dressed quickly and come down as the Oaklake elevator was afire. I dried myself as quickly as I could, dressed and went downstairs; before leaving my room, however, I gathered up all my hard-earned wages—my threshing money—63 dollars and the cheque received from Mr. Hatton which I had just cashed. As I was going downstairs the boss called out 'Hurry up, this place may not be standing in an hour.' I immediately went out into the back yard where I found the place as light as day and sparks flying around in all directions. My first occupation was to draw water from the well, enough to fill two pails. I went up on to the roof to see that the sparks, which were then falling like a shower of rain, did not ignite the felt roofing.

I was able to get from the roof a birds-eye view of the whole scene. The time was between 9 and 10 at night but everything could be seen as plainly as in the middle of the day. Two elevators, the Farmers and the Dowd were looking the same as usual but the third was enveloped in a mass of leaping flames and sparks and burning ashes were thrown up to a great height, and dropping all over the town, on the lumber yard, on the livery stable roof, on the hotel roof, in fact everywhere for a wide radius around. In front of the burning pile was gathered a big crowd who a few minutes previous to my appearance on the roof had been engaged in pushing the huge freight cars along the siding away from the fire. On many of the house tops were people busy keeping the lava from setting afire their homes. The night was very still, there was not a breath of wind, and it was intensely cold. Meanwhile the flames made short work of the elevator and it now was tottering from side to side, and at last with a mighty crash a great part of it caved in. The crash was followed by a tremendous shower of sparks for a few minutes. But the fire was still very great and it was thought that the gasoline store room would be likely to explode.

—*Noel Copping*

Fire engine

June 18th, 1910 was a red-letter day in the annals of Bulyea Municipality. At about 10 o'clock the quiet commercial air of a Saturday morning was suddenly broken by the loud clang, clang of an alarm bell. Forthwith some half-dozen stalwart men, prominent citizens of Bulyea, emerged from the CPR freight shed drawing the new fire engine—a brilliant object of shining metal and red buckets. The fire brigade under the directorship of a certain stout gentleman, a demonstrator sent specially for the occasion, towed the prize up the Main Street and presently broke into a stately run.

—*Noel Copping*

Vermilion fire hall,
c. 1913

Section gang

Monday, 24th January 1910: Started work as a navvy on the line. Tuesday, Wednesday, Thursday, Friday and Saturday I worked on the line. Work on the section seemed very hard at first, and the wretched influenza which I thought I had thrown off showed itself as soon as I began to do muscular work and gripped me in every part of my body. The first few days after the work was over I was aching in every limb and dog tired, and all the week the cold still kept with me, so on Sunday I stayed in bed all day.

The Bulyea section is about eight miles in length and the foreman has to see that the track is always in good condition. Besides myself there was also another fellow working under the foreman. We travelled up and down the track on a small car which was manipulated by means of a sort of pump. On this we careened up and down the tracks, usually west in the morning, and after dinner we went eastward unless we happened to be dining at Strassbourg, when we always went over the east portion first, and then went in the direction of Strassbourg. The first day we spent part of the time erecting rude fences to keep the snow from blowing on the tracks. We also changed a rail. Most of the time we spent altering the breadth of the tracks where the rails had spread or been drawn in too much. This was done by first cleaning away the snow then drawing the spikes which kept the rail tight down against the sleepers; the holes were then filled with wooden plugs and afterwards the spikes driven back. Then we had also to tighten the bolts on the joints, and spent nearly a whole day doing that alone. In some places where the tracks were not level shims had to be placed underneath the rails to raise them. When a train approached, our car had to be hauled off the rails until the train had passed. I, of course, was very green at this new job and very awkward at handling the tools. At first I found it very difficult to hit the spikes with the maul.

15th February 1910. Pay Day. Received my first cheque from CPR for work during January. During the last two weeks of February a sudden drop in the temperature which fell to between 35 and 50 degrees below zero. Some days piercing cold winds, while on others the air was almost still but the cold most intense. On the railway there was little or no protection from the elements. I got my nose, the lobes of my ears and both cheeks frostbitten. My hands often felt cold in thick mitts. The sun presented a strange spectacle—usually a sundog on each side of it, and sometimes one right above. One day, about an hour before sunset, it was surrounded by a faint ring of light which passed through the dogs; another ring seemed to pass right through it and encompass the whole horizon, getting fainter as it got further from the sun; a light tongue of flame seemed to shine upwards from the sun. During the last few days of the month we were visited by a blizzard and we had difficulty pumping along the track as the snow had in some places drifted over the rails. When we approached a drift we pumped our hardest to get through it. Sometimes we succeeded, but often we had to get off and push the car, and on several occasions we had to dig the snow away before the car could pass. Two or three times the car was derailed.

—*Noel Copping*

189

The St. Johns II: The land company business

Mr. J.F. Luse had at one time purchased a small amount of land in Dakota and settled it with Iowa farmers. He liked the business of colonization and when he heard of this vast unsettled territory in western Canada, he made a thorough investigation which resulted in the purchase (1903) from the Canadian Pacific Railway, of a tract of land lying along the 'Soo Line'. He purchased an old sleeping car, renamed it Ienza (in honour of his daughter), and proceeded to bring settlers into Canada. Through his sales, this rich land became quite popular and as these purchasers spread the gospel throughout the middle western States, the interest in Canada increased. Although incorporated under Canadian Laws, for convenience the head office was located in St. Paul, Minnesota, and more land was purchased.

During 1904 when the Luse Land Co. excursions arrived at Milestone or Wilcox, Mr. Luse made it a practice to bring his prospective purchasers out to our homestead, where they could visit with a pioneer farmer who had once been a bank teller. They would ask endless questions, to which I replied with that sincere faith I had in the soil and the future of Canada. This seemed to make a deep impression.

In the early spring of 1905, while working in the field, I observed a team approaching. It turned out to be a messenger with a telegram from Mr. Luse offering me the position of manager of his company. This offer was promptly accepted and I took charge. We proceeded to organize the company, on a colossal scale, by the appointment of over five hundred agents throughout the central and middle western States, and streamlined the operations to modern methods, many of which we originated. We appointed only men of good standing and character, many of them country bankers in whom the people of their communities had confidence. It was the agents' duty to call upon the farmers whom they knew to have a high financial standing with means to invest. Thus the agent knew how much land each of his prospects could buy and pay for. We did not run sight-seeing excursions, with the chance that some of them might buy land. Ours was a business proposition and the agent accepted as a prospect only those who earnestly sought investment. Thus, by the time our

excursions reached its destination I knew about how much land each man could buy and pay for. It was not our policy to sell a man more than he could pay for nor did we encourage the purchase of land for speculation. We were colonizers and much preferred the man who would move onto his land and improve it, for then we knew his land would eventually be paid for. Another thing that discouraged the tourist was that we charged each prospect his full railroad fare and one dollar and fifty cents per day for his berth and meals. If he bought land this would not be refunded, but credited on his purchase. Often in the excitement of a large crowd buying land, someone would get over enthusiastic and want to buy more than I knew he should, and sometimes it took more than a little diplomacy to convince a man that a quarter section of land was a good investment and not a whole section which he knew he couldn't pay for.

The size of these excursions varied from one to five or six cars. In the latter case they would be made into a train with a dining car attached and run as a Luse Land Special. Often during the rush season we would have as many as ten cars with over two hundred people when the train would be run in two sections.

The land was sold on a five year contract, one-fifth cash, the balance in five equal annual payments, with the privilege of paying any part, or all, at any time. The contract bore six per cent interest. We sold ninety-six per cent of our prospects, ninety-five per cent of which moved onto the land themselves or provided a tenant, with full equipment. If for any reason a purchaser was unable to assemble enough of this world's goods to carry out his part of the agreement, we took the land off his hands at no loss to him. It was not our policy to abandon a purchaser as soon as he had bought, but to give him every assistance until he was settled on his land.

A large portion of our land was purchased from the Railroad Company at three to eight dollars per acre. We were unable to buy land from the Government. They preferred throwing land open to homesteaders, which in later years proved very expensive for the taxpayers of Canada. Our operations spread over a large territory—along the Soo Line from Yellowgrass to Rouleau; the Tramping Lake District, operating from Scott, where we built its first building, before the Grand Trunk Pacific had reached the town, hauling the lumber from Battleford; the Little Manitou Lake District operating from Lashburn; the Humbolt District, operating from Dana—all in Saskatchewan. And also in the

Lethbridge District, operating from Magrath and more than three quarters of a million acres around Stettler, Alberta.

These activities had much to do with the settlement of the 'Last West' and we did not ask or receive any financial aid or concessions from the government or anyone else. We invested our own money, paid cash for the land, and brought in experienced farmers to occupy it. We left no one for the Canadian government to take care of.

—Seward St. John

People who Seized the Main Chance

S.T. St. John was born April 20, 1865, in Eldora, Iowa. Thirty-five years later he arrived at a tarred-paper shack on a Saskatchewan homestead. His list of tangible assets ran something like this: Buildings: one tarred-paper house, size 12 x 14 feet; one sod barn. Stock: one white horse, one Jersey cow, twenty chickens. Implements: one plow, one harrow and a meager supply of smaller tools. Cash on hand, $2.35. All this was twelve years ago. Today you can find S.T. St. John in a mahogany furnished office in Winnipeg as secretary and general manager of a company whose work it is to develop the hundreds of new towns throughout western Canada now being established by Canada's great Transcontinental Railway—the Grand Trunk Pacific....

The homestead has grown to a half-dozen larger farms; the tarred-paper shack to a resplendent home in Winnipeg. The dozen years are punctuated with a succession of rises—homesteader, manager of a lumber yard, manager of a land company, on up to his present height.

As the manager of a land company he personally sold more than 3,000,000 acres of Canadian land to American farmers. Considering the average size of each farm sold to be 320 acres, or half a section, and that seventy-five per cent of the purchasers became actual settlers, his work has brought more than 7,000 families to the Canadian West. This record alone is remarkable, but add to it the fact that he has yet to hear from the family who has regretted the move it made.

These achieved results were largely responsible for the organization of the company of which he is now chief.

As the railways are built the towns are established by the railway company, who are, so to speak, god-fathers to the towns. Coincident with the building of the Grand Trunk Pacific there was an inrush of hundreds of thousands of settlers into the new country opened. The establishment of hundreds of new towns became absolutely necessary to supply the needs of these settlers. The work of establishing these towns and to show opportunity-seeking men and women throughout the world the opportunities they offered became a huge task, so huge that a man was sought who could head a company whose work should be the development of these new towns and nothing else. The man who loomed largest on the horizon was S.T. St. John, and today in his office you may see a map of the world studded with cloth-headed tacks, each tack marking a town from which has come a merchant, manufacturer, homeseeker or investor he has influenced to become identified with the progress of some new Grand Trunk Pacific town of western Canada.

Not only has this man met with phenomenal financial success, but he has become rich in the esteem of men throughout two continents. His business and home life is an inspiration to the man who has gone down to defeat—fighting, yet who retains confidence in his ability to 'come back'.

—Opportunity Magazine, March 1913

Land company sale

Michael bought half a section of land from an American real estate company at 16 dollars an acre. The company returned his last instalment with in a notice that they were in no position to grant him a clear title for the simple reason that they possessed no title themselves. He was told to wait for some time. He waited for three years in vain. At last he had to buy the same land for the second time from another company, also American. The offices of the two companies were located in the same building, really in the same room. Michael paid a Regina lawyer 825 dollars but this did not help him any. One Saskatoon lawyer took 50 dollars also helping him in no way. A similar loss was sustained by six other farmers in the district.

—J.S. Woodsworth, 1917

Middlemen

When the railroad came in 1904, laying the last few yards of track on the flat prairie surrounding Melfort so as to be able to bring the first train in on time, things began to wake up. Two or possibly three elevators sprang up alongside the track. At threshing time loaded wagons could be seen crawling into town from every point on the compass and rattling home empty, hastening to get another load before nightfall. The wagons were not always empty. Grain cheques meant new purchasing power for the farmer and the newly built stores were fast bringing in stocks. Housewives were making demands on their share of the money earned and bringing more comfort into their homes, and the men, realizing that the true source of all this newly acquired 'wealth' came from the soil, splurged out in an orgy of implement buying that must have gladdened the hearts of the implement dealers in the new towns. Hammers could be heard day and night, all along Main St., as the freshly arrived merchants, hotel men, livery stable operators and the like worked furiously to get their premises ready for the harvests that were to come. On the farms, too, building was going on apace. Frame buildings were replacing the old log buildings with the sod roofs; better houses were springing up to replace those which, in their time, had seemed good enough. All this was the direct result of the grain cheque, coupled with the comforting knowledge that, as each succeeding harvest poured its golden burden into the hoppers of the elevators, more cheques would be forthcoming and there would be more things to be had.

Of course, prosperity is not always what it is cracked up to be. Merchants are not always doing business for the sake of their health, or, for that matter, for the complete good of the community they serve. Prices are not always kept within bounds; the slogan 'fair dealing and a fair profit' is not always adhered to. So the farmers, meeting in their schoolhouses, at church, at picnics, would turn their attention away from the fields and crops and explore the new subject of marketing. Why should a man pay, say, 10 cents for a pound of wire nails, when a 100-pound keg could be bought at Eaton's in Winnipeg for less than half that amount? Farmers rarely had any 'carry over' cash in their bank accounts. Notes given in spring for machinery had to be met—with tremendous interest charges—in the fall. Grocery bills even piled up waiting for the hoped-for flood of wealth when harvest was over. The banks in those days were 'easy'. Money to tide a man over, or to buy more land, or to increase his acreage under cultivation, or add to his herd of cattle, was generally forthcoming—at eight per cent interest—and the farmer, often as not, with but one thing in mind, to get the money, would sign a statement at the banker's polished desk that left him in bad case indeed if weather, early frost, drought or other unforeseen event should deprive him of his crop. Some men farming in those days were no doubt shrewd men; surely it is not for me to say that we were all careless, or even a bit dumb when it came to business matters, but just the same, before co-operatives, the Grain Growers Association and other co-operative enterprises took shape, the average farmer was very much at the mercy of what he delighted to call 'the middle men'.

—*Philip Crampton, Carrot River Valley, Saskatchewan*

Cars

The first cars that I remember seeing in the district made their appearance in the years just prior to the Great War and were owned and driven, mainly, by townspeople. The doctors, the lawyers and many of the merchants soon were seen far out on the country roads spinning along at the alarming speed of 35 miles per hour, or, often as not, encountered digging themselves out of mudholes or being pulled to safe ground by some amused farmer. It was about this time too that a boom in prosperity struck the west and Melfort, being situated in what the real estate men loved to call 'The Bread Basket of the World' was not slow in taking advantage of this new plum to be picked. Land adjacent to the townsite was bought up by newly formed real estate companies, subdivided into town lots and put on the market without delay. Many of their prospective buyers were looked for in eastern cities and more than one luckless investor coming west to inspect his lots found them miles from the town proper and as often as not staked out in some alkaline slough unfit for habitation. But for the real estate men—and how they increased in those hectic days!—it was great fun and the spirit of speculation soon spread to the merchants and even the farmers. Talk at the livery barn and hotel lobby swung sharply from grain prices and crops to lots and 'values' and easy money . . . .

A few farmers joined in the game and took a little fling at town lots. I well remember being driven around the outskirts of Melfort by one of these prosperous real estate men in his new Ford coupe. The roads were abominable, full of potholes and mostly detours around mud holes, but the dignity of this new prosperity had to be kept up, so drive it was. I did not fall to the blandishments of this newborn real estate tycoon at that time but later did buy a couple of corner lots on a street which I thought 'might some day' become a main thoroughfare, and gave nearly 1,000 dollars for them. Just what I gained from this investment I really don't know, unless it was some kind of comradeship among the other investors which singled me out as a man to talk property values with . . . . The summer crawled on and with the increasing heat the tempo of real estate gambling rose to a crescendo until my 1,000 dollar investment had risen to well over 2,400 dollars. We had just received our first tax notice from the town of Melfort and were surprised to see that our two lots were assessed at the tidy sum of 3,200 dollars. No doubt the town council was in a speculative mood too . . . .

So we hung on and dreamed dreams until the slump began to rear its ugly head. One day I was approached by an automobile man who had recently come to town and was seeking a suitable lot on which to set up business. Our lots were really just what the man wanted. He offered to give me a 960 dollar car in exchange for the property. I hung out for the 50 dollars or so difference between the car and the original price paid for the lots. It was a deal. I took possession of my first car the following day. I would have taken it right then so thankful was I at getting out from under what I had come to consider a white elephant.

—*Philip Crampton*

Curtis Road, Portage la Prairie

Edson Tennis Club, 1912

Prince Albert banquet, c. 1905-1910

Visiting

Several times during the summer months we must take a trip to town for groceries, at this time Billy was called into action. If we got away by 8 a.m. we would get into town in time for dinner. Then followed a delightful afternoon. If there happened to be a train due, we were taken down to watch it come in. As it drew into the station with the porter in his white jacket, the smiling trainman and the conductor in the background with women and children from far-away places peeping out at you through smoke-stained windows, it was a sight to thrill the heart of any small child.

Then there was shopping to be done in Calquhoun's Store. What a delightful place that was with wooden jam pails filled with strawberry and raspberry jam. Sometimes mother would buy one of these with a box of soda crackers. Then we knew we would be allowed to open them both on the road home and have jam spread on crackers when we felt the pangs of hunger. The happy anticipation was almost more than we could stand! Mr. Calquhoun with his beaming face and Scottish accent was an uplift to the spirits and always there were Indians—lots and lots of them. Mr. Calquhoun would insist that his wife would be dreadfully offended if we 'didna' call and see her. She lived in a beautiful stone house surrounded by large trees. She was small and looked a bit like Queen Victoria. The accent and regal surrounding made me think this was Dumbarton Castle. If it had been, I am sure I could not have been more awed.

Then there was Lottie and Jack Stuart who must be said 'hello' to. Mr. Stuart was the blacksmith of the town, and a fine smithy he was too. Sometimes it was necessary to have a horse's shoe fixed, or a wheel straightened before commencing the long ride home. I can still see his delightful smile as he recognized us and came away from his forge with his black leather apron on and his face streaming with perspiration from recent toil, while in the shadows of the shop stood a horse looking back over its shoulder, wondering at the delay and patiently waiting to have the work being done on it resumed. These were old friends, interested in the community and pleased to hear that life was going well in the south, as so it was with them.

—*Edna Elder*

J.C.F. Brown's Residence

199

Edwin Gibson house,
2nd Ave. E. & 10th St.,
Prince Albert,
Saskatchewan,
c. 1906

Calling

I prepared for my first calling day with great thoroughness. I swept and dusted. I polished the black stove, legs and all. I put out fresh stand covers, removed the fur from under the bed, and put out the best marseilles bed spread—coloured spreads were unheard of. I washed and ironed the pillow shams and carefully adjusted them on the wooden bar. The pillow shams were one of my prized possessions, and were one of my wedding presents. One was embroidered with a beautiful child asleep on a pillow of roses, on the other the same child awake, still buttressed with roses, and the inscriptions read: 'I slept and dreamed that life was beauty' on number one, and on number two, 'I woke to find that life was duty'!

I washed the morning-glory lamp shade and polished the gold acorns. I washed door knobs, polished floors, straightened pictures, made the table small, and put on a white linen cloth embroidered in violets. This embroidered cloth was my own effort and I hoped nobody would look at it too closely.

To Mrs. Ruttan, who was my guide and friend, I went for final instructions. What should I give my callers to eat on this first day? She said a cup of tea and a piece of wedding cake was the correct thing, but that looked pretty skimpy to me, so I added some home-made candy and still the table looked bare, but Mrs. Ruttan held firm. I must remember that the ladies were only calling—it was not a party.

But having cooked for threshers I had a fear of running short, and so made a loaf of sandwiches, cutting them so thin and small they looked foolish. But I knew that a thick sandwich would constitute a social error. I balked at cutting off the crusts, though . . . . I was very glad that I had the sandwiches for the callers came that first day in such numbers that if my good friend Mrs. MacNamara hadn't gone down the back stairs and across lots to her own house to bring me a full-sized chocolate cake, the news might have gone abroad that the bride had failed to provide enough food.

—*Nellie McClung*

Parlour and dining room

I thought nothing could be more beautiful than the satin-striped wallpaper on the parlour and dining rooms, one stripe plain and one flowered. The centre table had a cover of Irish crochet with raised pink roses, given to me by one of my pupils. The boys around town had given us a parlour suite, upholstered in Turkish design, each piece a different colour. A hanging lamp was suspended from the high ceiling and was raised and lowered by manipulation of two chains ending in gold acorns, the shade, of frosted glass, was patterned in wild roses and morning glories and was finished with a glass fringe which jingled when Adam McBeth's dray passed below on the street.

We had two pictures framed in oak, lovely sepia pictures of farm houses set in hilly country that ran to the sea, with cows on the meadows and curving roads leading to their rustic gates. The long windows had Nottingham lace curtains in a fern pattern, hanging from oak poles. We had two Brussels rugs and a fine oak dining table and chairs. In the kitchen we had a good, square, black stove. It had a good deep firebox and a fine oven and gave us assurance . . . .

—*Nellie McClung, 1896*

Mrs. Wilmott's drawing room, 1902

Jim and Claude Parkinson,
Kamsack, c. 1908

Diamond residence family at afternoon tea, August 1906

Band

The band from Brandon, with their great brass instruments, drove into the picnic grounds in their big democrat with red rosettes on their horses' collars, and when they alighted, coming swiftly down over the wheels, we were pleased to see how young they were. It was just a Boys' Band that had come to play for us . . . . They played 'Rule Britannia', 'The Maple Leaf Forever' and 'God Save the Queen' in a perfect torrent that shook the ground. I had never heard a brass band before and it affected me powerfully. It seemed to change everything while its billows passed over me.

—Nellie McClung, Clearing in the West, *p.111*

Town Band

In the evening the town folk were favoured with another procession, but of an entirely different character. No more was heard the rude clanging of brazen fire bells, but in its place rose the sweet, symphonious sounds of a village band. This institution under the leadership of Mr. Jocelyn was organised and formed sometime during the spring. What, though some of the rustic bandsmen were out of step and others out of tune—'let not ambition mock their lowly toil, etc., etc.' Here was a body of men of all nationalities and creeds, some farmers, some townsmen, drawn together by the influence of music.

—Noel Copping

Fair

Friday, 29th July. At about 8 o'clock in the morning I stood waiting on the station platform in company with several other section men and a number of townsfolk, for the CPR Special Excursion which was to convey us to Strassbourg. It being Strassbourg Fair Day we were taking a holiday. The train arrived at length and we were soon stepping out at Strassbourg station to be confronted with a town dressed in its holiday garments. The streets were bedecked with bunting gaily flying in the wind and along the sidewalks on the band headed a procession to the fair grounds, which lie north about half a mile of the town. A motley crowd followed, some on foot, some few on cycles, some in motor cars and the great majority in waggons, democrats, buggies. The first event of the day was stock judging, and this continued up to noon. There was a very good show of horses, cattle, some poultry and samples of this year's crops were also exhibited. After noon everybody adjourned to dine in town for the midday meal, and the people of Strassbourg were kept busy for a while supplying the wants of several hundred hungry excursionists. After dinner the grounds again became crowded with spectators to witness the trotting races. Baseball was played between Southey and Govan. In the evening the Strassbourg Amateur Dramatic Club presented a two-act comedy, *Uncle Rube*, the performance taking place in the Town Hall. I, however, did not constitute one of the audience, and with Arnold, Finlay and George, I spent the time until the arrival of the train walking up and down the main street, occasionally entering a store and disbursing coin of the realm on ices, drinks, etc. The others drank beer—I took nothing stronger than ginger ale with a little drop of sherry wine to flavour it. The train left Strassbourg at about 10 o'clock, and this ended the day's jaunt.

—*Noel Copping*

Picnic

Down by the river the tables were set and benches from the boarding house brought down for seats. There were raisin buns and cinnamon rolls, curled like snail shells, doughnuts and cookies (ginger and molasses), railroad cake; lettuce cut up in sour cream, mustard and sugar, cold sliced ham, home-cured, and mother had made half a dozen vinegar pies, using her own receipe.... She made her filling of molasses and butter, thickened with bread crumbs, and sharpened and flavoured with vinegar and cinnamon. Her one regret was that she had not the white of an egg to make a frosting, but we had no hens that year.

The great surprise of the day was the box of oranges that came from Rapid City, and a great bunch of bananas just as it came off the tree, held up before us by John Brown, the storekeeper. There were not enough to give one to each person, but we all had a piece, and what a disappointment that first taste of banana was! It tasted like white flannel to me. But in the barrel of supplies from Brandon was a wooden pail of chocolates, bell-shaped, black grocery chocolates....Two of these were our portion and having eaten one, and found it to be like something one would dream of but never taste, I tried to keep my second one to help me to meet some of life's viscissitudes. But looking at my treasure I discovered it was melting and spreading and oozing out between my fingers. So to save it I had to eat it. But I made it last as long as I could and licked my fingers so hard I almost took the skin off them . . .

The seats from off the wagons were set around the place where the baseball game was played. The ball was a homemade yarn ball and the bat a barrel stave sharpened at one end, but it was a lovely game and everyone got runs.

There were enough provisions for supper. So we stayed on and ate again, and were sorry to see the sun going down in the west. Coming home as we did at last in the purple prairie twilight, we were very tired and happy, with the pleasant evening sounds around us, drowsy birds softly twittering, the distant rumble of wagons, dogs barking, cattle lowing, the western sky still barred with crimson and bright-edged clouds above us; we were sure that no neighbourhood had ever had a happier picnic.

—*Nellie McClung,* Clearing in the West,
pp. 107-110

Minnedosa Fair, 1912

Town picnic

More than a hundred people are already there, and others are arriving, settlers in buckboards, Indians on ponies, and some on foot, all shouting salutations. Everybody is bubbling with enthusiasm for the big day. The lemonade booths begin to do business. Soon a game of baseball is organized. It is between the married men and the bachelors. Captains are picked, grounds paced out, and the game begins. There is not a glove nor a mask in the outfit. Gloves! Mask! Pooh! When these boys played ball they played *ball*. No sissies. Just he-men. The bachelors take the field. Fat homesteader goes to bat; he pounds the plate viciously, and swings like a windmill. Pitcher winds up and unwinds and shoots. The ball sizzles straight at the batter's head. It connects, and he bites the dust. The next batter swings at a wild pitch. The ball sails off out of sight. After a long search it is found in the pocket of a cherubic boy. The game resumes. The batter lams one out and runs to the wrong base, then heads for first, but is caught between bases. He dodges like a rabbit, but is finally hit in the ribs with the ball and declared out. The crowd cheers the good play, and the game goes on. The pitcher goes wild, and they get a new one. The boys hit him all over the place and score twenty-three runs. The married men then go to bat, and stay there till the other side gives up.

Lunch after the ball game. Sandwiches, angel cake, railroad cake and pie. Custard pie, apple pie, lemon pie, cherry pie, gooseberry pie, and every other kind of pie. Help ourselves; there's more where that came from. The food all soon disappears from sight.

Any other athletics? Most certainly. There is broad jump, foot races, high jump and pole vault. The sports announcer calls for a ladies' race. Fifteen soon face the starter. Their total avoirdupois is about a ton and a half. Stocking feet, bare feet, dimples and creases, what a display of ankles. Starter calls 'One, two, three, go.' The mass moves, breaks, and elongates. Parts of it trip and fall. Sally McGuire leads the field; followed by Mrs. Stone, a chin-length behind. Sally veers her bulk in front of her adversary, and holds it there until she staggers under the wire, an easy winner. . . .

The dancing begins. A fiddle jerks out the notes of 'Turkey in the Straw'. The artist scrapes the old fiddle till it howls, and bangs the floor with both feet, in a one-two, one-two, one-two beat. Couples line up for a square-dance. Red blouses, christy stiffs, jack boots, moccassins; long hair, bald heads, and water-falls. The caller intones, 'Honah yo podners. Corners the same.' See them step! They prance and caracole, double shuffle. 'Balance to yo podner; swing the corner lady. . . .' It's a whirlwind; you can feel fanning skirts twenty feet away. Thus the dance passes through the first and second sets, then the hoe-down is called. 'Places all. Hit the lumber with your leather; circle stags, and do-se-do.' They hit, they pound it and scrape it. They jump and crack their heels. Then, 'Right hand to podner; promenade to you know where.'

Down by the river, under the shade of the trees, another attraction is drawing a small crowd. Joe Morriseau is selling rot-gut at a dollar a bottle, and three drinks for a quarter. Fill the glass, or take just a splash. Great stuff! Holy Moses, how it burns! 'Have one on me this time.' Gasp and shudder, but put it down.

The long cool shadow of the western bank steals across the scene, and covers the picnic. Sunset: the evening chores await at home. Mothers, leading tired and whimpering children, begin to gather at the wagons. The big day is over, especially for sober-minded married folk. Our oxen are hitched, and we start for home. The animals step out brusquely, their minds on the home manger, but the long steep hill slows them. They finally reach the top, and plod on. A grey mist fills the hollows, and dew dampens the grass. Then the hordes of mosquitoes launch their attack. They pounce viciously on us, sticking their lances into every exposed part of us. Our arms, legs and necks become one big battle ground. We fight them grimly all the way. Home at last! A big smudge is started. The foe retires in sullen defeat. We 'hit the hay' tired and sleepy. The big day is over.

—*R.W. Dunlop, Foam Lake,*
Saskatchewan

Manitou 'salads' team

July 1st celebrations,
foot races, 1901

Greek Orthodox church and Russian contingent for overseas service, 1914-18

6
War

War

I never saw such a crowd at the station to see us off that day! Some of the enthusiastic soldiers off the incoming train from the West, whom I had organized into units, were unable to control their feelings. They hoisted me on their shoulders and I was borne triumphantly down the train. And before we left, I received a flask from my local doctor, a bouquet of flowers from a small girl in her father's arms, and a prayer book from my church presented by the Archdeacon.

It was a never forgotten farewell and a final farewell for many that boarded the train that day.

The train sped eastward into the night and stopped at various points to pick up details of men. At Moosomin the 5th battalion had also acquired a mascot, a goat with large horns and a long beard. It was immediately christened 'Sergeant Billy' as it appeared in Part Two orders. There had been many mascots among Canadian battalions, including 'Winnie the Bear' that belonged to the 2nd Brigade.

The general response to mobilization at Valcartier had been gratifying. The camp was filled with 2,000 officers and a brigade of infantry, more than required for a division.

Upon arrival in camp, I was temporary commander of the 4th battalion of the first Infantry Brigade (eight companies). This was made up of contingents from 35th Light Horse, Red Deer; 22nd and 29th Light Horse, Saskatchewan; 101st Regiment, Edmonton; 21st Hussars, Medicine Hat; 23rd Light Horse, Pincher Creek and 31st Horse, British Columbia.

—George Tuxford, Moose Jaw

Goodbye

In my diary I wrote that day, December 4th, 1915:

'This morning we said good-bye to our dear son Jack at the CNR station where new snow lay fresh and white on the roofs and on the streets, white, and soft, and pure as a young heart. When we came home I felt strangely tired and old though I am only forty-two. But I know that my youth has departed from me.

It has gone with Jack, our beloved, our first born, the pride of our hearts. Strange fate surely for a boy who never has had a gun in his hands, whose ways are gentle, and full of peace; who loves his fellow man, pities their sorrows, and would gladly help them to solve their problems. What have I done to you, in letting you go into this inferno of war? And how could I hold you back without breaking your heart?'

—Nellie McClung, The Stream Runs Fast,
p. 155

Prairiedale Red Cross

In January 1915, I organized one of the first Red Cross societies in the province, known as the Prairiedale Red Cross Society as we had no town near us. Our house from then on became the centre of Red Cross work and the Patriotic Fund, of which I was secretary. A bit later overseas parcels were sent from here to the boys in France. All that winter and all through the war we all helped get up entertainments, collect money and make garments for the Red Cross and other things. In all we raised over 3,000 dollars for patriotic purposes.

214

2ND CONTINGENT OF SASKATOON'S BRAVE BOYS

Looking east from 1st Avenue along 21st Street, Saskatoon, 1915

World War One

With the news came a swift and sudden change in the atmosphere within our home, quickly spreading through the community and in turn widening again to take in the entire country. It was as if the comfortable blanket of tranquillity and complacency that surrounded our contented way of life had been rudely lifted and the chill wind of danger from far-off places was allowed to seep in, until we suddenly became aware that it was also our danger! A new note crept into the murmuring of churchyard chatter. Boys who had never been thought of as being particularly courageous or patriotic were suddenly no longer there.

As is always the case when the morale of a people must be kept up—new songs began to appear on music stands. 'Tenting tonight on the Old Camp Ground' may have been suitable for past wars, but this was different. (Or so we tried to make ourselves believe.) We sang 'Keep the Home Fires Burning', 'We'll Never Let the Old Flag Fall' and 'Pack up your Troubles in your Old Kit Bag' with a gusto that was made more enthusiastic by the fact that deep in the heart of everyone lay the knowledge that 'Dying Tonight on the Old Camp Ground' still remained the true picture of war.

Nevertheless, the days went by quickly and glamorously too. It became a common sight to see trains loaded with soldiers, at every window a khaki-clad figure. Activities were directed toward raising money for the Red Cross. Concerts were put on. Patriotic and war songs enacted, such as 'Good-bye my Blue-bell' and 'Rule Britannia'. Recruiting officers in smart uniforms appeared, picturing life in the army as something to be truly desired. With the recruiting officers came the recruiting songs, and girls would sing:

'Come on Sandy, come on Jack. We'll guard your home 'till you get back.

'Down your tools, and leave your benches. Say "good-bye" to all the wenches.

'Take your gun, and may God bless you. For your King and Country need you.'

At one such concert, a young chap with a very fine voice and a twinkle in his eye, brought the house down by singing, 'Sister Susan Sewing Shirts for Soldiers'. A little Englishman, who was truly a comedian went as a stretcher bearer. Within the year the poppies blossomed for each of them.

Casualties were published and the papers were filled with names. 'Killed in Action', 'Wounded', 'Missing', were terms that became very familiar. With the casualties came the sob songs like, 'I didn't raise my boy to be a Soldier'. Another that appealed to me went something like this:

'So-long my dear old lady, don't you sigh. Come bid your grown-up baby boy good-bye. Somewhere in France, I'll be dreaming of you. You and your true eyes so blue.'

A small child with a good voice would come on the stage and sing:

'I want to kiss Daddy good-night. I want him to hug me up tight. My prayers have been said, but I can't go to bed, until Daddy has turned out the light.'

To my adolescent mind this was all very exciting and certainly proved a stimulus to the imagination, at the same time it didn't close my eyes to the tears that rolled down cheeks of mothers and the grim faces of fathers when these songs were sung.

Once I happened to be on a station platform when a train came through. I had always thought of the coming of a train as a joyful event—not so this one. No one got off, all blinds were drawn, the trainmen moved with a quietness and seriousness of expression that was indicative of sadness in the load they carried. We were told it was a casualty train, returning patients to hospitals within Canada.

—*Edna Elder*

216

Off to the front and good wishes for our soldier boys, Winnipeg, Manitoba

The Somme

ON ACTIVE SERVICE
WITH THE BRITISH
EXPEDITIONARY FORCE

April 28, /15

Dear Mother—

By this time no news will have been good news, and you will be pleased to know that I came through the recent operations alright. The latter I know will have been made well known in Canada. It was certainly a great experience and one I will not forget shortly. The Canadians will have still more to be proud of now.

Just at the time of the advance the weather was very disagreeable and continued so for some time after. It was surprising to see how the men can adapt themselves and stand the exposure, which was considerable during this move. We had very little shelter sometimes and what we did have we might have to prepare at night, dig a hole out in the side of a very wet and muddy and badly battered trench with a sand bag and rubber sheet for protection. A good many of the men suffered from foot trouble. I was bothered a little this way myself but otherwise I was free from colds and all the other ailments. When we did get out in billets for a short time we built some good fires and toasted ourselves and spent a good deal of our time in the blankets. It is funny to see two or three of the boys go down to a canteen, get a tin of herrings, a can of fruit and some biscuits then find a quiet corner or some isolated spot then thoroughly enjoy themselves as much as if it had been a banquet or great celebration in normal times. This is all for this time.

'John R. Gaetz'
19th Bat. Canadians

Dec. 12, /16

Dear Mother—

We had our first experience in the trenches and are now out in billets. At present we are in the infantry as there are no openings in the machine gun section.

The part of the line we are on is quite quiet and very suitable to get broken in. Harry Ellis and I are in the same company and occupied the same dugout.

The billets we have now are quite comfortable, well sheltered and we have stoves so that we keep warm and dry. Most of us are suffering a little from colds. I suppose it is on account of not being used to the exposure. It is certainly quite a change from Blighty. I have heard that what we left behind in England is now under quarantine.

Well I am in with a good bunch of boys, mother, and so far have received the best of treatment and am well looked after. And I'm glad to be able to take my place here for you folks at home so don't worry or fret.

I received a parcel, a Xmas box from you all and several letters and you may be sure I was greatly pleased over each donation and each letter. From now on I hope to be able to write once a week regularly as I will be more settled.

'J.R. Gaetz,'
19th Canadians, France

Galician

Look here! Our boys respond to the call of this country and enlist. But do the English respect them? No, not at all. They point to them with their fingers and say 'Look, there is a Galician in the uniform of a British soldier' and then laugh at them. I don't know why we should fight for them if they laugh at us.

Ladies knitting group, c. 1915

Mr. and Mrs. Charles Smith,
Pincher Creek Alberta
c. 1895

Private J. Smith
of Pincher Creek, Alberta,
who was killed in France,
August 1915

Postscript

That autumn (1919) we all had another crop failure. 1920 and 1921 proved the same. People, now completely discouraged, began moving out of the district. The crop failures each year were the direct result of lack of rain or moisture at the critical time when the grain was filling out. The land would just bake and burn up and the heads of wheat would whiten and curl over. Some years the grain would head out when only a few inches high and then die off.

During the war the farmers had all been urged to increase their stock and produce more of everything with the hope that the coming harvest would prove successful. Many farmers borrowed sums of money either from loan companies, who took the land as security, or from the bank, who took stock as security. The fall of 1922 brought no relief, or crop. The pioneers of the district were being harrassed by loan companies or banks who wanted money—the farmers could not pay. In many instances the land and the stock was being seized. It seemed as if there was a panic among the farmers. Some fled like thieves in the night leaving their land and stock for the sheriff. Others had sales. The stock and farm implements which the pioneers had secured at such high prices during the war were now being sold for next to nothing. And they themselves moved to more favoured districts. . . .

Now it was a peculiar coincidence that all the soldiers who had gone from this district lived on sections of land almost adjoining, forming a block north of us—our son Paul and Albert Walpole were the only soldiers who returned. . . . In May Albert went into a granary and hung himself. . . . For six miles square Paul and ourselves were the only ones left. During the past year 54 families have left the district. Paul has left. All the younger folks have gone. And we are left here almost alone, with sections and sections of deserted land around us, and we are getting old and grey.

—*Barbara Brent*

Weaver children, Saskatchewan, 1920

223

Credits

PHOTOS
Archives of Saskatchewan: 21, 25, 42, 87, 91, 93, 101, 107, 121, 125, 129, 135, 147, 165, 175, 176, 197, 201, 204

B. C. Provincial Archives: 51

Glenbow-Alberta Institute: 15, 19, 23, 30, 37, 38, 39, 45, 54, 59, 61, 63, 67, 71, 79, 81, 111, 117, 127, 137, 143, 145, 148, 155, 161, 164, 172, 177, 181, 185, 187, 196, 220, 221

Manitoba Archives: 20, 35, 47, 55, 65, 85, 126, 133, 140, 141, 149, 153, 167, 169, 171, 183, 189, 195, 207, 209, 211, 219

Meyers & Company, Photographs: 217

Notman Photographic Archives, McCord Museum: 95, 97

Page Toles, Toronto: 17

Provincial Museum and Archives of Alberta, E. Brown Collection: iv, 31, 33, 46, 60, 99, 103, 105, 113, 123, 130, 131, 151, 154, 163, 173, 179, 193, 199, 200, 203, 205, 212

H. Pollard Collection: 41, 49, 89,

Public Archives of Canada: 12, 22, 26, 43, 139, 158, 215, 223

MANUSCRIPTS
The majority of the excerpts in this book have been taken from unpublished letters, diaries, manuscripts and interviews in the collections of Canadian archives and foundations. Following is a list of the archives where the complete papers or manuscripts are available:

Glenbow-Alberta Institute, Calgary, Alberta

Georgeen Barrass, interview with Mr. and Mrs. E.F. Hoschka / Roy Benson letters/ Jessie De Gear memoir / John R. Gaetz letters / Joseph Heartwell memoir / Monica Hopkins "Log Cabin and We Two" (manuscript) / Mrs. Charles Inderwick manuscript / Frederick W. Ings manuscript / Douglas James memoir / Ellen Lively manuscript / Edric Lloyd interview / W. Hill Metzler diary

Manitoba Provincial Archives

Julia Asher manuscript / Augusta Boulton papers / George Dragan, Stefan Dragan—interviews in the papers of W.J. Sisler / J. Allan Ewens manuscript / Mayer Hoffer memoir / Kate Johnson manuscript / Edith Lazonby manuscript / Mary Morrison manuscript / Charles Alfred Peyton letters / W. J. Sisler papers / J.M. Wallis letters / Mrs. Ed Watson memoir / Gertrude Winter memoir

Public Archives of Canada, Ottawa

Annie E. Noel Copping, "Prairie Wool and Some Mosquitoes" / Alice Rendell, letters / J.F.C. Wright papers

Saskatchewan Provincial Archives
Grandma Bellamy memoir / Harry Buckwold interview / Ray Coates memoir / Philip Crampton manuscript / Z.F. Cushing memoir / August Dahlman manuscript / R.W. Dunlop manuscript / Edna Elder, *Western Producer*, June-October 1961 / Maggie Hamilton, the Hamilton family letters / H.J. Halldorson memoir / P.S. Hordern interview / Charlie Kwan interview / Jennie Nichols interview / Dr. Patrick papers / James Rugg manuscript / St. John papers, including excerpt from Opportunity Magazine / Wilhemina Taphorn memoir / George Tuxford letters in "Tuxford of the Plains" by Fred Wilkes /
The unsigned excerpts come from essays submitted to a series of competitions sponsored by the Regina Women's Canadian Club. These essays are collected in the Saskatchewan provincial archives.

University of Saskatchewan Archives, Special Collections, Saskatoon

Barbara Brent manuscript / Clarence Butterworth manuscript / James Clinkskill manuscript / John Easton manuscript / Mrs. Ed Watson manuscript /
J.S. Woodsworth, "Report of an Investigation by the Bureau of Social Research, Governments of Manitoba, Saskatchewan and Alberta, 1917" (contains also report on Ukrainian school and quote from Canadian school ma'am).

BOOKS
Excerpts from the following books are reprinted with the permission of their publishers.

Zella Collins, *The Hills of Home,* Altona, Manitoba, D.W. Friesen & Sons, 1967. / Nellie McClung, *Clearing in the West,* Thomas Allen & Son, 1964. / Nellie McClung, *The Streams Run Fast,* Thomas Allen & Son, 1964. / D.E. McIntyre, *Prairie Storekeeper,* Peter Martin, 1970.